Radical Urban Solutions

Urban Renaissance for City Schools and Communities

Dick Atkinson

CASSELL

Cassell
Villiers House   387 Park Avenue South
41/47 Strand   New York
London WC2N 5JE   NY 10016-8810

First published 1994

British Library Cataloguing-in-Publication Data
A catalogue record for this book is available from the British Library.

Library of Congress Cataloging-in-Publication Data

ISBN 0-304-32828-6 (hardback)
      0-304-32830-8 (paperback)

Typeset by Colset Private Limited, Singapore

Printed and bound in Great Britain by Redwood Books, Trowbridge, Wiltshire

Other titles in the Cassell Education series include:

Chapter 2

The Scale of the Urban and Educational Problem

intro

The present state of our great cities is cause for public shame and disgrace. They are witness not just to pollution, ugliness, wastefulness and environmental eyesores, but also to economic catastrophe and spiritual disorder. The symptoms of urban discord and decay become ever more visible and intractable day by day with standards in both communities and schools being unacceptably low. Just how low they are needs to be detailed and their profound implications accepted.

HOUSING

Most of the houses which were built as towns expanded 100 to 150 years ago were still in use in the 1950s. Understandably, many were in some disrepair by then. The Government and most cities decided to help their urban communities by demolishing these old houses, in their place constructing twenty-storey tower blocks. At the same time, whole council estates were built in outer city areas, also comprising high-rise flats. These tall buildings were interspersed with rows of square, faceless, low-rise flats and houses. Large numbers of families who had lived in the inner areas were moved to these outer-area estates, leaving their old houses void whilst they awaited demolition. The old houses and the new flats which rose in their place were filled by newcomers. Immigrants came first from Ireland, then from the Caribbean islands, the Indian subcontinent and Africa.

The existing community was thus split up as huge population movements took place. It was as if large parts of the inner areas were physically picked up by some unseen hand and scattered around the new outer-ring council estates. The elderly and the infirm were often left behind to adjust to a new life with newcomers from other continents. The new estates generally failed to provide either social amenities or personal gardens for people to tend, with most open spaces in the new estates being public. No one felt that they owned them so urban geographers coined a new phrase to describe them, calling them 'confused spaces'.

David Hargreaves (1982) invites us to consider post-war Newtown in Liverpool, which rapidly became one of the most

vandalised housing estates in Britain. Some 10,000 homes were built there in nine years and the population grew to 60,000. As part of the slum-clearance drive in Liverpool, families were wrenched from the old inner-city working-class communities in Scotland Road and deposited in new estates some miles from the city centre. Kirkby was given the nickname 'Bunnytown' since at one stage nearly half the population was under fifteen years of age, giving it the highest child population in Europe. It is a telling index of the place's distorted social constitution. The old extended families had been broken beyond repair; many men were unemployed or had to commute to Liverpool to work. Vandalism was not confined to the young; some council tenants began to damage their own accommodation in the hope that the council would be forced to find them alternative housing. No doubt the local politicians and planners had the highest ameliorative motives, but their ignorance of, or disregard for, the realities of social structure and culture had disastrous consequences. As one observer expressed it, 'over one hundred years of cultural tradition was dismissed without apparent thought'. The social clubs and working men's clubs closed, the Boys' Brigades were disbanded, the corner shop became vandalised and empty.

The idea of 'wholesale slum clearance' in the 1950s and 1960s was replaced by the concept of 'urban renewal' in the 1970s and 1980s. The planners had been persuaded that it was wrong to demolish houses wholesale and split up entire communities only to replace them with spiritless new estates. It seemed more sensible to demolish only the very worst houses to create more open spaces and to renew every house which could be repaired in order to keep families together. Even so, the occupants of each house in the terrace to be renovated had to leave for temporary residence elsewhere while their old home was gutted and reconstructed. Again, the intention was good. It seemed an improvement on the previous approach, but many moved out permanently rather than face the disruption. Those who remained suffered two decades of disruption and dislocation, while sites remained derelict, and houses stood void and open to further vandalism. Not every builder was scrupulous, for upon returning to their improved house a family too often found that it still suffered from damp and a host of faults which took years to rectify. Also, just as had happened in the outer estates, confused spaces grew like mushrooms. The intention was good: the space created by a demolished corner shop was grassed and planted with a few trees; a road closure was marked by a raised flowerbed; front gardens of converted houses joined the pavement and road without the benefit of fence or wall. However, within weeks these confused sites attracted litter, weeds, discarded furniture, uncollected plastic household rubbish bags, rats and stray dogs. Renewed inner-ring areas quickly came to look as desolate and uncared for as the outer-ring estates.

EMPLOYMENT

The number of people out of work began to rise in the 1970s. Throughout the 1980s and the early years of the 1990s the number without work fluctuated between 1,500,000 and a peak of 3,500,000. By the end of 1993 it was nearly 3,000,000. This meant that over 10 per cent of the potentially employable population were not working. These bald figures mask the fact that in some areas of our cities this statistic rose sharply to 40 per cent, while in the case of youth unemployment it often stood as high as 80 per cent.

Until recently, people were shocked if unemployment rose above two to three per cent. Once, most people could expect to hold down a manual labouring job in one or

other of the manufacturing industries. Today, the decline of these industries means that few traditional labouring jobs exist. The new technological industries which have taken the place of the old ones require a higher level of skill and training and fewer pairs of hands. Once unthinkable, a high level of unemployment now appears to have become almost inevitable. This spells a low level of morale for the traditional bread-winner, a life of strain and anxiety for the family and a social environment which is not conducive to a child's development. What has this child to look forward to? What kind of ambitions are realistic targets to aim for? They say that hope springs eternal. For the child in a family which is affected by unemployment it is too often a sour dream.

THE FAMILY

Young and Willmott's study (1957) of changing family and kinship patterns in East London in the 1950s told a universal tale about the disruptive consequences of demographic changes which were leading to the reduction of the size of the family, and how the family was further being torn apart by housing policies and patterns of work. Once, the extended family had included grandparents and other relatives who lived in close and supportive proximity. Both family and street had provided continuity and stability for young parents and their children, and dignity for the elderly. As the family slowly became reduced to the nuclear one, containing just two adults or even one, the mutual support of close relatives was removed. Whilst modern technological inventions such as the refrigerator, washing machine and TV made life less physically hard, the quality of that life and the nature of social support suffered both at home and in the street.

The change from the extended family to the nuclear one has made it more difficult for parents to raise their family without the strain showing and adversely affecting their children. Relaxation in the law has made divorce easier and it is now much more common. This may be thought to be the easiest and most liberal solution to family strain, but from the child's point of view it can be the hard option. The rise in the number of single-parent families illustrates most pointedly the fact that the family is under serious threat. Once, the child born to the single parent bore a mark of social disgrace which brought its own handicap. Now that this moral stigma has been largely removed as a result of changes in values, it has been replaced by other even more debilitating social and economic ones.

The Office of Population Censuses and Surveys (1991) reveals that the number of single-parent families in Britain has doubled in the last twenty years. More than one in five children are now born outside marriage. In 1971 the total number of one-parent families was 570,000. But, by 1989 the figure had become 1,150,000. In 1988, one in six of all families with dependent children was headed by a single parent. In 1989, an estimated 1,900,000 children were being raised by one parent. This was double the figure for 1971. Figure 2.1 tells the tale in starkly visual terms.

The total number of live births in 1990 was 706,000. This was three per cent more than in 1989, which was the highest total for eighteen years. But, while births inside marriage increased by only one per cent, the increase in births outside marriage rose by as much as eight per cent or 200,000.

The 1991 census figures show that 32.6 per cent of children in Inner London come

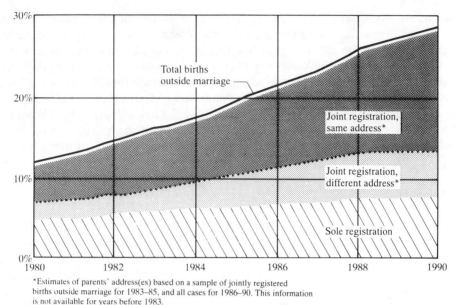

Figure 2.1   *Live births outside marriage as a percentage of total live births in England and Wales.*
(Source: Office of Population Censuses and Surveys (1991))

from single-parent families. In Lambeth the figure was 41.6 per cent. The figure for
Liverpool was 32.7 per cent. Anthony Bevans (1993) suggested that these figures reveal
a 'relative collapse in the traditional concept of the family; the married couple with
dependent children.'

Of course, many single parents cope well and endow their children with advantages
beyond those enjoyed by some born within marriage and whose parents stay together.
But, on average, both single parent and child have a much more difficult time. The child
is more likely to be sickly and to die early in life. The child is likely to do less well at
school and, if male, to be tempted into a life of crime. The child is more likely to become
an unemployed adult and, if female, in turn to become a single parent.

Some people are surprised to discover that the children of divorced parents who
remarry do not fare as well as the children of parents who remain single. In 1991, Dr
Kiernan, who is research director of the Family Policy Study Centre, said that 'the risk
factors associated with divorce and remarriage are . . . highly significant and demand
further investigation.' Children of parents who remarry leave school and home earlier,
cohabit and marry at a younger age and become parents sooner than children of single
parents, let alone those who are children of stable marriages. A study of 17,000 children
by the Policy Study Centre which was published in 1991 clearly showed that children
faced more upheaval through the remarriage of a parent than they do when their parent
stays alone. For example, stepdaughters were twice as likely to leave school at sixteen,
twice as likely to become teenage mothers and four times more likely to marry before
twenty. Not only did the avenues to further education of both boys and girls become
closed but they also had poorer career prospects than other children. Malcom Wicks,
who is the director of the Study Centre, said: 'Any notion that divorce has been a

Likelihood that children from divorced families will:

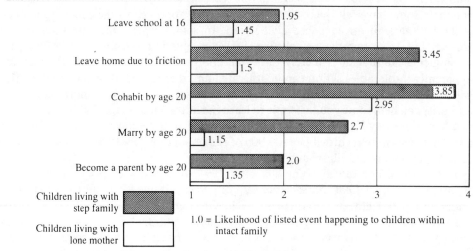

Leave school at 16	1.95	1.45
Leave home due to friction	3.45	1.5
Cohabit by age 20	3.85	2.95
Marry by age 20	2.7	1.15
Become a parent by age 20	2.0	1.35

Children living with step family

Children living with lone mother

1.0 = Likelihood of listed event happening to children within intact family

Figure 2.2 *Effect of family disruption on young adult life.* (Source: Family Policy Studies Centre)

bloodless revolution and that children are resilient enough to survive divorce without lasting disadvantage is clearly shattered by the results'. They are tabulated in Figure 2.2.

In February, 1993, Professor A. H. Halsey questioned several decades of social policy when he said: 'We're arriving at a situation where the man never arrives, never mind leaves. There is a growing population of children born into single-parent families where the father has never participated as a father . . . and from the missing father flows the missing community ethic.'

SELF-CONTROL AND AUTHORITY

Today, neither the family nor the community are resilient enough to agree a consistent moral code and exert a common authority, which a child needs in order to develop self-discipline and respect for adult authority. Of course, young children do not at first know how to control their passions, and seek instant gratification by crying and attention-seeking behaviour. Their last resort is the temper tantrum. Many families gradually manage to help their child to learn the social skills required to gain self-control and the ability to defer gratification to a socially and morally acceptable moment.

However, children who do not receive consistent, firm but loving control and discipline may never learn how to master their desires. They learn to pursue their objectives by self-indulgent, often bullying and violent means, which do neither themselves nor anyone else any good. Some parents, especially single parents and those dispirited through lack of work, suffer so much that they wash their hands of responsibility at the earliest opportunity, thus compounding the problem. As a result, authority figures in schools and other institutions can find themselves helpless in the face of young people who have not learned how to discipline or respect themselves.

This problem is made more acute because society as a whole has become more

ambivalent and relaxed about how it defines those rules which are essential for civilized conduct. Some have felt that a liberal, *laissez-faire* approach to the conduct of others is the hallmark of an advanced civilization. In some respects they are undoubtedly correct, but from another perspective, however, this is far from the case. For, the 'delinquent' can and does merely draw the unintended conclusion that their errant, apparently intolerable, action can be tolerated and that no moral or punitive sanction will be exercised. A generous, liberal or modern interpretation of moral codes and authority can help some young people to learn the mistaken message that selfishness and bad behaviour pay instant dividends. The statistics of crime have multiplied. In 1950, 1,000 offences were recorded per 100,000 of the population. By 1990, it was 10,000 per 100,000, as Figure 2.3 illustrates.

Just as the crime rate is rising sharply – 1991 witnessed a 20 per cent increase in reported crime over 1990, while 40 per cent of detected crime is committed by juveniles under the age of eighteen – so there is a decline in church attendance. While old prisons are overcrowded and new prisons are opening, traditional Christian churches are closing. Politicians are nervous when bishops claim the right to make comments about how everyday society should be organized. The politicians seem to ask that religious and moral authority should be confined to the consideration of the dwindling congregations of the nation's churches on Sundays.

Many are coming to feel that one contributing factor in the increasing rate of delinquency and crime is to be found in the decrease in the level and in the exercising of moral authority in everyday life. By this authority they do not refer prissily only to the code of conduct of the priest, but also to that of the 'older generation' and the 'police officer on the beat' and the 'teacher in a school' who were once the stewards of the tried and tested values of society. There is much evidence that the consensual grip with which 'adult authority' of various kinds once held in check the unbridled passions of young people has become so loose that at times it has little or no hold at all. 'No-go' classrooms and streets have graduated to become 'no-go' areas and communities. For every visible 'no-go' community whose youths have rioted against property, people and police, which thus hits the headlines and precipitates an unseemly squabble between priest and politi-

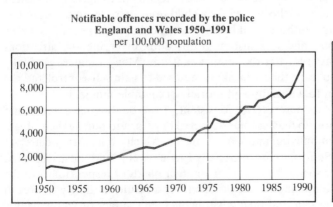

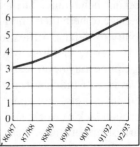

Figure 2.3 *The rising graph of crime – and of spending on the police.*
(Source: *The Independent*, 11 February 1993)

cian, there are also dozens of areas which no commentator notices. Yet each of these areas teeters on the brink and strikes unseen and unrecorded fear and foreboding into the hearts of most of their residents.

There is also the growth of what Ralf Dahrendorf, Charles Murray (1989) and Frank Field have referred to as a new kind of 'under-class' of young men who have never known work and of young, single mothers whose children are themselves destined to join this new under-class. Their analysis, the *Sunday Times* pointed out: 'will offend all those who hold the Conservative Government responsible for the new kind of poor in our midst – the street beggars, the young people who live in cardboard boxes, the homeless and the chronically unemployed.' Charles Murray's findings pose uncomfortable questions they would prefer not to face. His under-class has 'cut adrift from society and has no intention of rejoining it, no matter how generous the welfare state or how much well-off people are penalized for being successful. It is characterized by drugs, casual violence, petty crime, illegitimate children, homelessness, work avoidance and contempt for conventional values. So strongly is it taking root in Britain', says Mr Murray, that it 'could become proportionally larger than it is in the United States where it had a head start. In short, a social tragedy of Dickensian proportions is in the making: all the elements are there. The under-class spawns illegitimate children . . . and feeds on a crime rate which rivals the United States in property offences. Its able-bodied youths see no point in working and feel no compulsion either'.

They reject society while feeding off it; they are becoming a lost generation giving the cycle of deprivation a new spin.

The ambitious move

The 'under-class' make life less comfortable for the 'respectable' poor and the 'relatively' affluent. The distrusting relationship between them has the consequence that urban areas have quite literally become desolate. People may well manage to bother with their own house and backyard but feel that they can exert no influence over their street or wider community. They used to succeed. Then they tried and failed. Now they do not bother. The predominant feeling has become one of either isolation and retreat or 'I've come to long for the day when I can get out and live somewhere else'.

The most zestful and able achieve this ambition. According to 'population trends', people are leaving the cities and industrial conurbations to live in rural areas, new towns and resorts. The first results from the 1991 census show that 9 per cent of the population of Merseyside, a once great sea port and trading conurbation, had left since 1981. Some 5 per cent had left Greater Manchester and the West Midlands in the previous ten years. The fastest-growing counties were Cambridgeshire and Buckinghamshire. Those districts which were growing most quickly were ones such as South Hams in Devon and North Dorset, and new towns such as Milton Keynes and Redditch.

People move for a number of reasons, but the two factors which are of particular interest here relate to 'getting on their bikes' to search for work or to get a better job and because they are looking for a more secure and comfortable environment in which to raise their family. The communities which they leave behind are thereby made that bit poorer. The public reputation of such areas gradually becomes so bad that no one with similar ambition replaces those who leave. A vacancy is filled only by those who

are destitute, in difficult straits or immigrants to the country. The movement of the labourer from the countryside to the burgeoning manufacturing town of 150 years ago is in danger of going into reverse today as those who 'have made it' move out to rural commuters' villages, leaving behind those who are young or elderly or infirm or without hope. The downward spiral twists on apace. Less visible than some signs of urban decay, but more serious, is the fact that the spirit of too many families and the communities which surround them has been broken. Parts of towns have become like 'acultural deserts' in which residents have lost the confidence, the skill and the will to tackle the litter, graffiti and crime. The spirit needed to enable whole communities to become revitalized and develop afresh seems to be entirely beyond them.

For a child growing up in this atmosphere of decay and valueless insecurity, a real sense of potential and purpose must seem like a luxury which can only be glimpsed on the unreal screen of the television set. Quite simply, what can be the point of either hard work at school or ambition? The downward spiral is given its penultimate spin – almost to the point beyond which recovery is not possible. But still there is more. The final twist in this sorry tale of modern urban blight is cruelly given by schools.

EDUCATION

Schools, many of them built 100 years ago in the first flush of state 'elementary education for all', now look unwelcoming to teacher, pupil and parent alike. The paint is peeling. The broken windows and leaking roof remain unmended. The hedge is overgrown. The grounds are ill-maintained. Worse still, the standards attained within the school are low. Too many pupils are significantly underachieving. In 1991, in two areas of Birmingham 87 per cent of all children at the age of eight had a reading age below their actual age. Only 12 per cent gained a result in GCSE English. Only 8 per cent gained a result in GCSE maths. There were several schools in Birmingham in 1991 where every child was performing below his or her potential. These harsh statistics are given in Tables 2.1 and 2.2.

Table 2.1 *Reading age compared with actual age.*

	Two city wards	UK average
% of population with reading age greater than or equal to actual age (8 years)	13	50
% of population with reading age lower than actual age (8 years)	87	50
% of population with reading age two or more years below actual age (8 years)	31	20
% of population with serious difficulties (8 years)	10	1.3

Table 2.2

	Some schools	UK average
% of population with reading age lower than actual age	100	50

The deficiency which the primary school figures reveal in the performance of 8-year-old children becomes progressively worse as they get older, that is, the gap between the actual age and the reading age becomes steadily wider. This has a disastrous knock-on effect by the time these children are due to take their GCSEs at 16 years of age. A third of these children simply don't take any public examinations. In effect, these pupils leave school functionally illiterate and with a deep sense of failure. Far too many of the remaining two-thirds of the children aged 16 fare hardly any better.

A well-recognized bench-mark for measuring whether or not 16-year-olds have done well or badly is to note whether they have gained five or more GCSE passes with grades A, B or C (the old O level). To gain five or more means the pupil has done reasonably well. To gain fewer indicates a poor performance.

UK statistics show that only 31 per cent of all pupils gained this target in 1990. In Birmingham the figure was 23 per cent. This compares with other large towns whose children do equally badly. But these figures include the grammar and other 'good' schools, and if these were taken out of the statistics then the figures for most state comprehensive schools would be much, much lower. The facts are easily discovered in the case of Birmingham which has seven grammar schools. Once these seven grammar schools are removed from Birmingham's grand total of 76 secondary schools, the remaining 69 schools, 91 per cent of the total, have an average of only 16.7 per cent of their pupils who gain the target. That is, in the case of 91 per cent of Birmingham's schools as many as 83.3 per cent of pupils gain fewer than five GCSEs. Indeed, of these schools, there are eight where only 5 per cent or less of their pupils gain the target. In some 27 schools, only 10 per cent or less gain the target. In contrast, the seven grammar schools have an average success rate of well over 90 per cent.

On close examination, therefore, it is not sensible to concentrate on the simple arithmetical average of 23 per cent, for only a very unrepresentative total of two of the city's schools actually hit this average. It is more meaningful to look at the most commonly achieved sets of results. There are at least three sets of these results:

- 54 of the 76 schools got on or below the 23 per cent average. That is, 71 per cent got on or below the average.
- 22 of the 76 schools got above the 23 per cent average. That is, only 29 per cent came above.
- 60 of the 76 schools came below the national average of 31 per cent. That is, 79 per cent came below the national average.

The mathematical average of 23 per cent is thus seriously skewed by the city's grammar schools and those seven other schools which come above the national average. They are carrying the rest. Most pupils and most schools are seriously disadvantaged and underperforming. The rest of the country need not be complacent simply because Birmingham is not doing very well. The national statistic of 31 per cent is very poor. It simply demonstrates the fact that most state comprehensive schools in most cities do just about as badly as Birmingham's schools. A recent *Reader's Digest* survey (1991) of over 200,000 people in seventeen European States showed that Britain came 'bottom of the class' in two out of the three questions asked (Table 2.3).

This is why Sir Claus Moser, warden of Wadham College, Oxford, said that

Table 2.3   *Britain at the bottom of the class.*

Have faith in our education system (%)		Have a degree or professional qualification (%)		Left school by the age of 17 (%)	
Denmark	77	Sweden	58	W Germany	15
Switzerland	77	France	55	Denmark	20
Finland	77	Norway	51	Norway	23
W Germany	71	Austria	44	Sweden	28
France	63	Belgium	36	Netherlands	32
Norway	63	Netherlands	33	Belgium	37
Portugal	60	Luxembourg	31	Finland	38
Ireland	59	Italy	29	Austria	42
Netherlands	58	Finland	25	France	44
Austria	57	Switzerland	25	Luxembourg	47
Italy	55	Greece	24	Greece	51
Belgium	54	**Britain**	22	Ireland	52
Sweden	52	Portugal	21	Portugal	59
Luxembourg	48	Spain	20	Italy	61
Spain	47	W Germany	19	Switzerland	67
Greece	43	Denmark	19	Spain	69
Britain	37	Ireland	13	**Britain**	69

'Hundreds of thousands of British children have received educational experiences not worthy of a civilized nation'.

The original surge in educational standards which started 100 years ago when all children were first obliged to go to their brand-new schools has now slowed to such an extent that an intense debate rages as to whether standards are static or actually falling. In his Annual Report of January 1991, the Chief HMI (Her Majesty's Inspector), Eric Bolton, reported that at least 25 per cent of primary children were seriously under-achieving, whilst 50 per cent were of only 'average' attainment. The national ideal average which Sir (now Lord) Keith Joseph set when he was Minister of Education suggested that the typical child should be able to attain five good passes in the GCSE public examination at 16+. As we have seen, even this unambitious 'ideal' has not yet been attained.

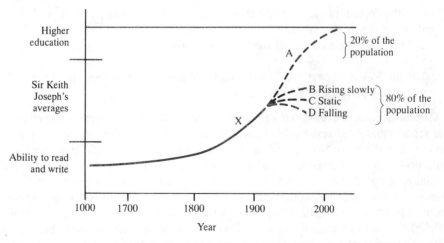

Figure 2.4   *A representational graph showing how standards should be rising (A) compared with where most commentators locate them (B, C and D).*

Heated though it is, today's debate about standards is misplaced. The argument should not be fought out between those who argue for one or other of the B, C or D options depicted on the curve of educational standards of Figure 2.4. Whether standards are actually falling (D), static (C), or still slightly rising (B), is a relatively fine, but uninteresting, academic point. It is akin to the equally inconsequential debate about how many angels can dance on the head of a pin. For it is quite clear that standards are no longer rising at anything like the rate they used to (X) or should do (A) if most people are to attain the standards of which they or our nation's competitors are transparently capable. There is no genetic reason why most people should not reach the same educational level as the student who enters higher education or its counterpart in Germany or Japan. This possibility is represented by Figure 2.3's A curve. Quite apart from the missed opportunity which this curve represents for the individual, it clearly reveals the substantial waste of a national resource. It also compares very unfavourably indeed with Britain's competitors. If the system was working properly the figures should reveal that after a hundred years of education for all, not a mere 31 per cent but at least, say, 80 per cent, were in higher education or staying in the 'system' beyond the age of seventeen. But the figure for the UK is stuck at 31 per cent while that for the old West Germany is 85 per cent.

The story is an even more depressing one than the statistics of failure, underachievement and low educational standards alone can convey. Children today do not just fail to do well educationally. They also fail to do well culturally. The drab environment, fading economy, poor housing, high crime rate and the high incidence of single-parent families and family breakdown all contribute to a malaise of the spirit, a sense of hopelessness which comes from a fractured, disintegrating culture. The poorly educated young people of today also have no firm, clear, culturally inherited yardstick by which to judge right from wrong, to give hope, meaning and purpose to life.

In this sense, they are doubly deprived. Having failed to gain an adequate education, they have also failed to gain an essential means of evaluating, ordering and shaping their life. There is little need to wonder why on several occasions in the 1980s the nation and its politicians watched in uncomprehending horror while Brixton, Toxteth, Bristol and Handsworth burned.

GOVERNMENT

Whilst blaming each other for causing Britain's problems, the political parties appear merely to have attempted to manage the decline of the nation rather than to steer a visionary new course. Indeed, the parties appear to suffer many of the symptoms of decay themselves. Barry Hinds and others have recorded the decline of working-class politics and, indeed, the diminishing interest in politics and regard for politicians and political structures by people at all levels of society.

It is not just the public behaviour of some politicians which has led to this low public esteem. It is mainly due to the fact that the structure and organization of politics which grew from the industrial era is no longer relevant to the business of everyday life in post-industrial society. Fewer and fewer people participate in the political process except at the time of general elections. More significant, fewer and fewer people invest either faith or confidence in the process or its outcome.

In other words, at the very moment when people, the family, school, community and nation most need a strong lead, they cannot find it. There is thus a danger that government and the political parties are contributing to public ills and not alleviating them.

YESTERDAY AND TOMORROW

Crime rates were falling at the turn of the century even though the new manufacturing industries were creating devastating urban poverty. However, throughout the last half-century the nation has moved out of the phase of industrial growth and international stature. It has become unconfident of its role and its future. This chapter has described the range of ills which confront it.

A question arises: 'If this decline goes on, what will things be like in twenty or thirty years' time?' If the cycle of decay which became so visible in Britain between 1960 and 1990 continues to spiral downwards at the same rate until the year 2020 this nation, which was the first to industrialize, could become a truly fearful and squalid society. Relegated to the third division by its competitors, especially those from the East, it could come to qualify for 'underdeveloped' status as it enters a new dark age.

So people rightly speak of an urban crisis in Britain, which is no less acute in some other Western societies. They say that towns today are soulless and fractured places with which no one can identify. How can it have come to pass that in the midst of plenty there is such great pain and sorrow? Is the modern town necessarily a place which breeds fear and loneliness? Is this the inevitable result of an industrial past and relative affluence? Or, can something be done? If so, who are the people who will provide a better and more balanced way of living? What ideas will galvanize them into action? What kind of city could they build in the place of today's concrete jungle?

REFERENCES

Bevans, A. (1993) The *Independent*, March.
Birmingham LEA (1991) Advisors' Reports, Central Division.
Halsey, A. H. (1993) The *Guardian*, February.
Hargreaves, D. (1982) *The Challenge for the Comprehensive School*. London: Routledge.
Hinds, B. (1971) *The Decline of Working Class Politics*. London: MacGibbon & Kee.
Kiernan, K. and Wicks, M. (1990) *Family Change and Future Policy*. Family Policy Study Centre.
Murray, C. (1989) The Under-class. *Sunday Times Magazine*, 26 November.
Young, D. and Willmott, P. (1957) *Family and Kinship in East London*. London: Routledge.

Chapter 3

From General Problem to Particular Solution

All political parties now recognize the fact of urban blight. Indeed, education, employment and the environment top the political agenda for the 1990s. Many have tried to alleviate the problem. All the political parties first recognized in the 1960s that local government and town halls alone could not provide the impetus required to 'stop the rot'. After all, matters were getting worse despite the existing way of administering and running cities.

The Home Office started a programme of urban aid in the 1960s which was followed by a number of other initiatives, including the Department of Education and Science's 'Education Priority Areas' which were masterminded by Professor Halsey (1972) and practised most effectively by Eric Midwinter in Liverpool. Then came Community Development Programmes.

These early initiatives became enlarged into the Department of the Environment's 'Inner City Partnership Programme' (ICPP). The ICPP was launched in 1975 in grand style at a conference in Bristol sponsored by the Gulbenkian Foundation and the *Sunday Times*. It was attended by Labour's Peter Shore, the minister who was then in charge of the Department of the Environment, and Peter Walker and Michael Heseltine, who followed Peter Shore into that office. It was difficult to distinguish between, or fault, their caring and enlightened views. The great cities of the country were in real difficulty, they agreed. They were in the downward spiral of decay described in the previous chapter. The grand town halls, built at a time of civic pride and colonial expansion in Victorian times, were no longer able to inject new blood and zest into the huge cities which they now struggled uncomprehendingly to administer and manage. Huge sums of money had been poured into these cities in the post-war years in central government's attempt to make the whole country a 'place fit for heroes'. Inner city 'slum' terraced houses had been knocked down and new high-rise flats had been built in their place in inner and outer city areas. New, radial roads taking traffic into and out of towns, and circular ones which took it around them, had been constructed. New schools had been built to accommodate the still growing, physically healthier population. The existing post-war distinction between grammar and secondary modern school which entailed testing children at 11 + had been gradually phased out as comprehensive schools came

to symbolize an all-party consensual belief in 'equal opportunities'.

Yet, despite all this goodwill and honest intention something, somehow, somewhere, had gone so terribly, even totally wrong that the latest remedies seemed not to alleviate but to add to the ills and the blight. Those grand, well-intentioned changes seemed to be slowly, inadvertently, adding to the urban nightmare. Messrs Shore and Heseltine thus created the new ICPP form of urban aid to help local cities and central government spend their existing money in new ways which could breathe new life and heart into the decaying, uncared for urban areas. They argued that if all the post-war help which had come through the existing central and local government machines had had little positive effect, then perhaps it was time to use that money in different, fresh, more imaginative ways. At first, the idea was that this money should be spent in new city and voluntary projects designed to encourage the revitalization of communities. Successful ones would point the way forward and show how both city and central government could devise quite new ways of financing, administering and managing their towns.

This has not happened. Whilst relatively large sums have been spent year by year both on voluntary projects and on city programmes, very little of lasting worth has resulted. Bright stars have burst upon the firmament here and there. But the mainstream budgets, philosophies and ways of acting of the town halls and their major city departments have stayed largely unaltered. Those stars which still flicker do so despite, rather than because of serious city support. Even after all the good intentions and ICPP funding of Messrs Peter Shore, Peter Walker and Michael Heseltine it cannot be said that one inner city area, let alone one town, has been rejuvenated anywhere in the country. On the contrary, many costly and imaginative schemes have come to nothing, leaving in their wake only feelings of frustration, anger and a sense of hopelessness and despair. Valiant ideas and intentions were not backed up by adequate will, so the juggernaut of existing ways of doing things easily knocked them aside. Peter Willmott and Robert Hutchinson (1992) wrote that: 'After fifteen years, and many new initiatives, surprisingly little has been achieved.' They concluded their report for the Policy Studies Institute: 'Given the record so far, it is difficult to have much confidence in more of the same or feel at all hopeful about the future prospects for the deprived urban areas.' In recognition of this, Mr Heseltine persuaded the Department of the Environment to have one more concentrated effort to change things. He initiated the 'City Challenge' scheme in a serious attempt to co-ordinate central and local government resources to aid the recovery of key urban areas.

Over one hundred years ago, far-sighted city fathers set up town halls and created the new system of education for all. The times must have been exciting, even exhilarating. But the modern form of those creations it seems, has become part of today's urban problem. The world has changed and the once innovative town hall has become a moribund monopoly, immune to the concerns of its customers and incapable of responding to their needs. Worse still, the system has so anaesthetized the concerns and expectations of ordinary people that they no longer feel that they could help to put matters right. 'If the only system we have ever known and in which we have invested so much of ourselves cannot solve the crisis, it is surely absurd to suppose that we can do it on our own!' Or is it?

People are beginning to realize that the problem cannot be solved by throwing more money at it through the various departments of each town hall. If a solution is to be found, then the problem must be examined from a fresh perspective and existing

energies and resources redirected. At the very moment when some expected the hopes of two hundred years of progress to be realized it is necessary to rethink the very foundations on which our major cities have been built; their education systems and the way they cater for the individual and the family. A new adventure, the need to construct a new urban Renaissance, urgently calls.

CHARITY – THE FORGOTTEN FACTOR

The charity of which St Paul spoke had a universal and central significance to human life. By charity St Paul meant neighbourliness and wholehearted care and concern for people. He felt that it was not possible to construct family and community life unless charity was used as the basic foundation, 'Faith, hope and charity, but the greatest of these is charity'.

In modern life the concept and practice of charity has been pushed to the periphery of social life by the complex organization of society and the provisions of central and local government. The 'system', the State, now assumes the role of the provider of caring services. Charity now lives in the soup kitchen. It has become the long stop or safety net for those who fall through the otherwise monopolistic provisions of the welfare state. The concept and practice of charity is no longer a key aspect of the way of life for all. Rather, it is dispensed by a fortunate few to the unfortunate. The Salvation Army, the homeless who sleep under London's railway arches, or the starving people in a far-flung land are what most people now associate with charity.

Quite recently, however, a silent revolution has been taking place in the charitable arena. Its style has changed from doing things for the deserving poor to doing things with others and enabling people to do things for themselves. The last thirty years have seen a host of playgroups, nurseries, adventure playgrounds, advice centres, residents' associations, housing associations, tenants' associations and carnival committees springing up within communities in most cities. Their activities have waxed and waned because it has been difficult to find the funds to administer them properly and provide consistent support. Too often, therefore, that support has been of an amateur kind which has, perhaps, been provided by a vicar, a headteacher, a student in vacation time, or a college leaver working for a year in voluntary service before taking a 'proper' job.

Such charities and voluntary organizations have provided the catalyst which has helped residents in some urban areas to raise their sights for a while before funds ran out or a key figure left the area. Unfortunately, such bottom-up organizations have too easily been treated with disdain or ignorance by those who administer and have a vested interest in the established way of doing things. Until very recently they have been overlooked by Mr Shore's and Mr Heseltine's officers and their successors in their search for a challenge to the city which would lever serious change and fresh thinking into the corridors of power and the culture of the wider society. However, it is important to ask what effect such independent, voluntary, charitable effort might have if it could be injected with a high status and become professionally led. In other words, can it come to replace parts of and exist in real partnership with state-provided services?

It is useful to focus on one charity, St Paul's Community Education Project Ltd, which has operated for twenty-two years in Balsall Heath, an inner area of Birmingham. The difficulties which confronted Balsall Heath in 1971 when St Paul's started and

which it now faces are typical of those found in every inner area and many outer areas of the land. St Paul's is important, however, because while it is controlled and managed by local people who live in Balsall Health, it comprises not just a playgroup, nursery or carnival, but all these and many other agencies which together form an integrated set of community facilities. Together they are the size of a large city agency or school, but they are home-grown and independent of city provision. St Paul's started in 1971 with just £50, but its operating costs in 1992 had become £500,000, of which £100,000 was raised locally. At today's prices it represents an investment of £10,000,000 not just in Balsall Heath but also in an action research project which is bristling with implications for what might be possible elsewhere. Perhaps St Paul's can stand for and illustrate the kind of autonomous local service which every community needs if it is to develop a positive identity and pride.

REFERENCES

Halsey, A. (1972) *Educational Priority*. London: HMSO.
Willmott, P. and Hutchins, R. (1992) *Urban Trends*. London: Policy Studies Institute, July.

Chapter 4

St Paul's Community Education Project Ltd

Some 150 years ago, Balsall Heath was a small staging post just a mile from the very small town of Birmingham. In those days, Balsall Heath really was a heath dotted here and there with farms. Life was difficult, but the individual and family managed to shape most of their own life chances within the wider traditions set by the Church and the lord of the manor. With the advent of the Industrial Revolution Birmingham grew rapidly and the fields and heathlands of Balsall Heath became filled with row upon row of terraced houses. The area became part of the artisan heart of a rapidly expanding town as a whole series of villages became engulfed within Birmingham's urban sprawl. St Paul's church was built and later its church hall was constructed. They became thriving local points of communal and spiritual life.

As the town of Birmingham grew and the town hall was built, so the context of the life of the individual and family changed in areas like Balsall Heath. Provision was made from the public purse for the construction of local baths, a library, sewers and half a dozen local schools. This burgeoning period of growth in economic, educational and social life was shattered by the country's loss of the Empire which coincided with the loss of Birmingham's manufacturing base. As the original economic rationale for the existence of Balsall Heath disappeared the community became poor. In the 1950s and 1960s large numbers of residents left in search of a better life elsewhere. Their old houses became occupied by successive groups of equally poor and dispossessed newcomers from the West Indies, Africa, Pakistan and Bangladesh. These newcomers mingled with the few native residents who were too old, infirm, physically or socially handicapped to leave. By 1970 this mixture had become a recipe for misery and an anonymous existence which held little purpose and had no common aim. On Christmas Day in 1971 St Paul's Church had a congregation of six people. Its church hall had become empty and unkempt. By 1981, the national census revealed that the area fell within the most deprived 2 per cent of neighbourhoods in the whole country.

Balsall Heath now suffered the multiple deprivations discussed in Chapter 2. It had a desperate need for stability and growth, but they were not in sight. It had become a net exporter, not of goods and services but of problems. Its residents had once been independent, had shaped their lives and built their environment. Now they had become

dependent. They urgently needed the wheel of social harmony to be reinvented so that the bandwagon of a revitalized, spirited, community could start to roll.

ST PAUL'S NURSERY

In 1970 a teacher, the local curate, two parents and a trade unionist started St Paul's nursery centre in the empty St Paul's church hall. Local parents were desperate for a nursery place for their young children so that they could go to work or have a little respite to ease family difficulties. The nursery centre combines the hours and educational content of a nursery school with the extended day (7.30 a.m. to 6.00 p.m.) and the social and health care content of a social services type daycentre.

It has catered successfully for fifty children for over twenty years and has brought stability and purpose into the lives of many families. It is a place where a child who might otherwise not receive all the benefits of a stable, integrated, family life acquires the basics of literacy, numeracy and social co-operation and is given a head start in school life.

It is also a place which belongs to the community around it. During the evenings and weekends the building is open for use by community groups of all kinds who do not have premises of their own. We can leave the nursery centre, with the picture of one of the first children to attend returning at the age of twenty-two with her husband and their families for their wedding reception and the comment of an elderly visitor who had lived in the area before the last war who said: 'Goodness, it's just like it used to be.' What had been a church hall, then a derelict building has become not just a nursery but also a valued village hall. Young though it is, St Paul's has begun to acquire its own history.

THE COMMUNITY EDUCATION AND RESOURCE CENTRE

Twenty years ago children of all ages roamed the streets around the nursery centre at all times of the day and night. They had little but empty, vandalized houses and rubble-strewn, derelict sites to play in. They naturally teamed up with other youngsters and, as they say, the devil found work for idle hands. The drift into delinquency often occurred before anyone had realized it. The apparent excitement of housebreaking and car theft, the supposed relief from boredom in glue sniffing or petty acts of graffiti daubing and other vandalism, violence and bullying were understandable. There was little else to do without a more caring and intelligent leadership than that offered by peers, let alone without a more constructive and challenging environment than that offered by the drab urban townscape. It is a sad and surely avoidable fact that over 50 per cent of all crimes are committed by young people aged thirteen to eighteen.

If a child is given a torn piece of paper and a blunt pencil then he or she will not produce his or her best piece of work. With the right tools, encouragement and the knowledge that the end product will be well-mounted and proudly displayed for all to see, then he or she will try hard. The community and education resource centre started, like the nursery, on the initiative of just a few local people. It began as an adventure playground which opened only in out-of-school hours. At around the same time the city started two similar ventures in two nearby parks. Since those days St Paul's centre has

developed in response to local demand and through voluntary effort from what had been a derelict site once occupied by two rows of decayed terraced houses into a purpose-built complex agency which is open from 9.00 a.m. to 9.00 p.m., often later, six days a week and for forty-eight weeks a year. It comprises a hall, kitchen, craft and technology room, stables, allotments and a nature area as well as a floodlit sports pitch in addition to the original adventure play area.

The city's own two centres suffered a different fate. Their agenda was set in stone. Neither changed at all over the years. They became graffiti-strewn and dirty and the parks in which they were situated and the park users began to suffer. In 1988 and 1989 respectively these centres were burned down. The streets immediately surrounding both locations had become the sites which, if ever Balsall Heath were to burn, would provide the tinder and spark to ignite the whole area.

In its attempt to bridge the gap between school and home and to surround a child of any age with enough to occupy him or her, which is adventurous, stimulating and educationally challenging, St Paul's centre staff invited both home and school into its life. It has shown the school that it has much to benefit and learn from the home and community. In turn, it has shown the families that school is not the only place where education takes place. It is needed in everyday life. Writing, reading and arithmetic need to be refined and resourced by school because they are a key to success and achievement for an individual in the community.

To help it to play this supporting role the centre has attracted to its doors the dozen nearby primary schools, the two secondary schools and a sixth-form college which are all located in Balsall Heath. Pupils from all these agencies come in school hours to study at the centre. For them, education has become an exciting way of working on and in the real world in out-of-school hours. The centre acts as the playground for all the children of the area. If the nursery has developed the village hall of the area, the centre has developed its village green.

LANGUAGE ALIVE!

Just as the dozen schools in the community of Balsall Heath relish their visits to the centre, so Language Alive! moves out from the centre to visit them. For many local children English is a difficult, second language. For others, whilst English is their native tongue, mother and father do not always have the time, patience, confidence or awareness to encourage their children to overcome their difficulties and realize their potential. For these children and for their teachers the Language Alive! project became an exciting opportunity for recovery. It entails a small group of teacher/actors working closely with the class teacher and parents both in the classroom and in the community in ways which bring language to life through the use of participatory drama.

Dorothy Heathcote, a leading authority on theatre in education (1990) wrote:

Theatre always involves fresh ways of discussing and presenting matters. Usually, though, an audience watches and learns only a little. Further, there is normally no effort to link with the background and interests of those who watch. The little that is learned is only related with difficulty to what is already known. Theatre in education methods used by Language Alive! transform the children (and also the teacher and the parent) into actors, by drawing them into participation in programmes. Thus, words and action must be

considered, used, tested and reconsidered by everyone present at a presentation. Skills, concepts and ideas must also be explored by all. The project is the most active of learning experiences.

Theatre can be a stimulating and exciting experience which can help us to make sense of the world in which we live. Yet, all too often it is dull, boring and unrelated to the lives of children and young people in communities. Too often audiences are expected to act as passive recipients prevented from making an active response. The participatory theatre in education strategies used by Language Alive! challenge this ethos. Drama and role play are used to transform children and young people, teachers and parents into actors who are able to explore themes and concepts actively, learning through experience. It is this active participation which is central to the work of the Project.

It is just as valuable as an in-service training medium for teachers as it is a learning experience for children.

With the help of Language Alive!, St Paul's centre came to act as something like the voluntary hub of a wheel of statutory schools and the community. It attracts children to it formally in school hours and informally in the evenings and at weekends while also reaching out to schools, visiting and presenting them with an array of teaching aids.

ST PAUL'S SCHOOL

The nursery, resource centre and Language Alive! support pupils who attend nearby schools. St Paul's small secondary school started because existing staff and parents realized that some secondary-school-age children were simply not going to school at all while others behaved so badly that they were excluded from school. In 1973, three teachers and five families registered St Paul's School with central government's Department of Education as an independent school. While, therefore, it has the same independent status as Eton and Harrow, St Paul's School started in two empty terraced houses. Later, when a nearby primary school building became empty, the school negotiated its way into those premises.

Pupils who arrive at St Paul's have often been used to 'getting away with it' in the sense that nothing serious or too worrying has resulted from their actions. This is because parents either do not know or do not mind and teachers do not know or do not have the time to mind. Indeed, some parents keep their daughters at home quite deliberately because they need an extra pair of hands to help with housework. Some children have learned that a tantrum, sulk or other forms of behaviour are sufficient to cow or make indulgent a harassed parent. Equally, from a teacher's point of view, a troublesome pupil will not be sorely missed. The pace of school life allows no time for more than a swiftly penned letter home which might gain a fitful attendance for a while. Without a St Paul's school, the destiny of many pupils is to leave school without any public examination result at all, with a sense of failure and fatigue and an unformed intention to explain to their own children that school and education will hold no opportunity for them.

The staff at St Paul's quickly came to see that one way to deal with lateness or absence is to go home and fetch or to get the parent to bring the child. Any time or work missed is made up by detention and by staying as late as need be to complete it. Departure times of 5.00 p.m. are not unusual in the early days of a child's attendance until the lesson is learned.

Once a complete and clear determination to impose their will is shown by the school and home, with the help of a home–school contract, then the pupil normally comes into line. He or she is often helped in the process by older pupils who say: 'It's no use. We tried it, they just keep on at you. There's no way round it.' It is clear that firmness and discipline are respected, even admired, but sloppy and unfair application of discipline or any inconsistency can cause resentment. The same approach is applied to discipline in general with uncivil behaviour being dealt with immediately. If the act warrants it then detentions or other sanctions are applied. Parents or other relevant authority figures may well be told. Everyone is helped to draw the line so that what will and will not be tolerated is made abundantly clear.

When parents or figures in authority strive for friendship with children at the expense of exercising their authority they enter into what John Crook has imaginatively called a 'conspiracy of immaturity' which calls forth a response of contempt on the part of the child. Such parents and teachers fudge the clearly defined moral framework which young people need, and consequently postpone indefinitely the real friendship which can develop between adults and children who have grown up.

There is often a gulf between what children say they want, for their appetites can be quite limitless, and what they accept that they need. They need to know what the limits are, what rules they must live by. Provided these rules are fairly and equally applied they will generally be respected, and as important, the adults who enforce them will be respected. The resulting relationship of trust forms the context in which the ability to teach and excite can be exercised. The caring 'stick' of authority goes hand in hand with the 'carrot' of understanding and creating a warm, colourful, homely and affectionate atmosphere within the school.

Most children enjoy primary school. They are known and called by their first names. Their class teacher is with them throughout the school day, so they are known as individuals. The school is relatively small, perhaps with just three or four hundred in all, so it is like a small community. There are paintings on display, exhibitions of craft work and a warm, colourful feel to every room, corridor and door. St Paul's centre can help these children to sustain and retain their interest in their existing school, so St Paul's had no need to develop its own primary school. However, the break at 11+ is sharp.

Secondary schools are less personal places than primary schools. They are larger and their catchment area covers a far wider geographical patch. Every subject carries with it a different teacher and a different room. Despite all the many ways by which the secondary teachers care for their pupils, the child who is already slipping behind and is unconfident will slip further behind. It is easy to feel alone, isolated and unloved in the secondary school context and to develop an aggressive manner to hide the hurt. Several St Paul's pupils attended their previous school, answered 'present' to the roll call at the start of the day and then simply wandered the corridors. No one ever noticed that whilst present they were absent. Too many pupils simply give up the effort of going to school and stay at home or leave as if to go to school, then simply wander the streets. Often pupils who arrive at St Paul's have not seriously attended school for two or three years.

It is not surprising that the reading age of the 14-year-old is often 8 or less. Indeed, many things that the St Paul's pupil knew at the age of 8 have long since been forgotten by the age of 14. It is of little surprise to the St Paul's teachers that so many secondary

school leavers gain no public examinations and leave without a ticket to life. Worse, in place of that ticket, they have learned to positively mistrust and hate what they see as authority and education. Their eleven expensive years of state education have taught them only to distrust society and cover their hurt with the pride of defiance.

Whilst we saw that the national rate for achieving five GCSEs at grade A to C is 31 per cent and that Birmingham's average is 23 per cent, it is important to note that at St Paul's it is 50 per cent. A number of its pupils have gone on to college. Almost all have found jobs and recovered from the unfortunate situation they were in before they came to the school. St Paul's works. The first years of the school were very hard, but, as soon as even a brief history of success had been achieved it helped to create a tradition and culture which eased the path for newcomers, both pupils and teachers. The sense of belonging to a wider community which includes a village hall and green, nursery, resource centre and the Language Alive! project is important.

It has also proved important for the pupils to see their teachers grapple with some of the wider problems of blight in the area. They take pride in the fact that 'their' centre's farm stands where rubble once littered the ground. They enjoy helping the children at the nursery and assisting with jumble sales to raise extra finance. They note that their teachers who set standards for them within the school are also out in the community doing something about the environmental context in which they live. They know that the results are good so they see that what they would otherwise have felt was a 'soft and soppy' caring is muscular and brave.

If any large school is to be respected by pupils, parents and community then it must expel and be seen to expel those pupils who cannot or will not live by its rules or accept its code of conduct. While the large school is thus helped, the unlucky child is too often left to wander the street. Having acquired a serious negative label – 'bad', 'failure' – it is more than likely that more trouble will follow for both the child and whichever authority figure is encountered.

Even when the town hall provides an exclusion or suspension unit for a few such children, the labelling process has already done much damage and the process of recovery is difficult. 'If I'm seen as bad, I may as well live up to my reputation.' A key to the secret of the success of St Paul's is that it is a 'real' or 'proper' school in its own right and its pupils leave with the real ticket of exam success to the outside world. Therefore, it prefers to take its pupils from the large secondary schools before the final act of expulsion has actually taken place, so the message can be conveyed to the pupil: 'You are now changing to a smaller, good school which can pay special attention to your particular needs and you will succeed.'

Some children have learned from their family and street that the 'best' way to gain attention is to make a thorough nuisance of themselves. Such children can stop a large school in its tracks and destroy its reputation unless they are removed from it. Small schools, like St Paul's, are needed to relieve the large schools and to rebuild the confidence and self-esteem of children who otherwise would become a menace to themselves and everyone else.

A further key to St Paul's success is that this small (40 pupils), 'good' and 'normal' school is also surrounded by a community of 'extra-curricular' community activities, the nursery, the resource centre and other pursuits. Added to close links with home, and the knowledge that St Paul's also has its firm code of behaviour to which the home has assented, these complete the St Paul's equation.

THE COMMUNITY NEWSPAPER

Balsall Heath gets a very bad press. The rest of Birmingham has developed a reflex action which goes 'Balsall Heath equals bad news'. For most inner and outer city areas this is a familiar problem and it depresses the children and their parents. They do not want to be told that they live in a slum. This causes those who are able to do so to leave or to send their children to schools which are outside the area. St Paul's staff and management committee decided that a way of countering this problem was to produce a local paper for the area. They called it *The Heathan*. All the local good news which only local people might recognize is written up each month and presented with attractive photos in a twenty-four-page newspaper. Once a term *The Heathan Educational Supplement* is inserted into its centre pages. This is also sent to every home in the community via pupils in the primary schools.

The paper is supported by advertising from local firms and by sales. *Heathan* sellers from St Paul's, including its school pupils, knock on every door in the area to distribute the paper. They also send it to every city councillor and a number of people whose opinions, decisions and actions can help to change the image of the area to 'Balsall Heath is beautiful'.

HEATHAN ENTERPRISES

The printing press which produces *The Heathan* is occupied with that task for only one day each month. A full-time printer is fully occupied every other day of the month printing school magazines, residents' newsletters, church notices and letterheads. *Heathan* Enterprises has become a valued community facility which enables all local agencies to raise the standard and tone of their communications with each other. It inspired one young person to set up his own desk-top publishing business which functions both commercially and as a community enterprise.

THE COMMUNITY ENTERPRISE CENTRE

The newspaper and printing business have led to the supply of other, potentially commercial services to nearby schools and the community. For example, with the help of volunteers and work-experience schemes St Paul's removes graffiti from gable ends, and public and private buildings. It clears derelict sites of rubble and litter. This scheme developed into a painting and decorating squad which began to improve the appearance of local schools, their entrances and exits as well as their classrooms.

The community enterprise centre's activities have proved to be a most interesting, financially significant development. For, though independent, the nursery, resource centre, and school are dependent on city and charitable grants. But, the community enterprise centre is able to sell its wares to other agencies. It behaves less like a charity and more like a trading company with the potential to generate enough income to cover its own costs and make a contribution to other parts of St Paul's.

THE COMMUNITY CENTRE

All the St Paul's buildings are used in the evenings and weekends by a wide variety of groups – English as a second language classes, an Asian elders day centre, bands, scouts, badminton and volleyball, religious ceremonies, wedding and engagement parties and residents' groups. The buildings really have become the village hall of the area. It is in this context that staff and volunteers and community figures organize two area-wide social functions, a carnival and a bonfire.

The carnival is deliberately held before the schools in the community break up for their summer holidays so that they can all become involved. Care is taken to encourage them to build their contribution into the term's work. Thousands of residents and their families participate in the two-week long event which has become an occasion for celebration. It is certainly one of pride. In a community which is already united, say, a rural village, then perhaps a religious festival such as Easter or Christmas might be the moment when the whole community comes together to express its faith in itself and its future. In the case of Balsall Heath that moment is the carnival.

Bonfire night as traditionally celebrated in the UK generally coincides with the Hindu festival of Divali, so it is possible to combine the two occasions in one. A huge fire, stalls, acts, a small fair and a magnificent firework display now attract as many people as the carnival. It has become the second moment in the year when the community can come together and gain strength from a joyful act of solidarity as it prepares for the winter months.

The bonfire and carnival are moments when this once decayed inner-city area which, to outsiders, represents crime, conflict and insecurity demonstrates that 5,000 people can assemble for long periods of time and police themselves with the help of just two police officers. The nation still marvels at the solitary policeman on his white charger who long ago was able to control the massed football fans at Wembley. It is important to note that he could still do so in Balsall Heath.

To get to this point, some fairly traditional, good, old-fashioned concepts had to be hauled out of the cupboard, dusted down and proclaimed afresh in the context of today's needs. Achievement, quality, standards, hard work, neighbourliness and faith are not easily explained to everyone today, any more than to the errant St Paul's pupil. But the task had to be undertaken before Balsall Heath could raise its standard and declare itself to be on the road to recovery and begin the 'Building a Better Balsall Heath' campaign.

ST PAUL'S INDEPENDENT MANAGEMENT

The staff of the project need the parents and their neighbours to help in a variety of ways. These include:

- To push and encourage their children, so that home and school are pulling in the same direction and to ensure that no contradictory message is given to the child.
- To help with jumble sales and other local fund-raising activities.
- To act as extra pairs of hands so the clubs, teams and farm are efficiently organized.

- To assist with the management and policy formation of the different parts of the project and the overall board of directors.

Because this help is so clearly needed – if it was not given the staff would be on their own and flounder – it is gladly given. If beyond St Paul's lay a city department the context would be different, the need not apparent, the help grudging. The independence of the project has called forth a sustained and substantial response from the area.

St Paul's is both a charity and a limited company. Its locally devised and approved constitution incorporates the requirements of the Companies Act as well as those of the Charity Commissioners. It holds an annual meeting to which the staff and directors report. All those living or working in the area are entitled to become members and to attend and vote at the annual meeting. The main function of this meeting is to receive the company's written report and accounts and to elect the next year's board of directors and ensure that the project is in touch with the needs and wishes of its membership. Though drawn from people living and working in downtown Balsall Heath these directors manage a complex agency which not only looks after many local children and sustains a series of agencies but also supplies support services to a dozen nearby local authority schools which are valued by them more highly than the city's own services. St Paul's has even begun to supply some of these services to clusters of schools in other parts of the city.

COMMUNITY DEVELOPMENT

The staff and management committees of St Paul's nursery, resource centre and school soon discovered that no matter how much progress they made in the school day all their good work could be swiftly undone overnight, at the weekend and in the holiday time by unsupportive aspects of the community. Even the most excellent teaching could not withstand cramped living conditions, leaking roofs, a raucous TV competing with homework, arguments which flow from the frustration of unemployment, a desolate environment and negative peer and adult role models who signal that school and education is not relevant to the real world of home, street and the community.

The cavern which yawned between school and street easily engulfed all the efforts, good intentions and spirit of teacher, child and parent. The only solution which made sense was for the staff of the project both to teach well and to reach out to the growth and strong points within the community to ensure that they became resilient enough to overcome its negative features and to support the efforts of school.

The activities of the community centre, newspaper and enterprise centre were crucial in this respect. However, even they were of no significance on their own. The whole project found that it had to approach all the residents' groups, mosques, churches, schools and businesses within the wider community and propose the need to 'Build a Better Balsall Heath'.

It became necessary to align the apparently separate disciplines, professional interests and city departmental boundaries of housing, recreation and the police so as to enable them to pull together in harmony with the efforts of the project and community. Of course, each distinct professional area and the city and other agencies had their

own special demarcation points. It had to be carefully explained to each that their interests could not be satisfied if they confined their action only to the narrow boundaries of their specialism. Just as St Paul's staff could achieve more if they became involved in the development of the wider community so too could other professionals who had previously been lodged in their own particular enclave. The political parties were not exempt from this but they, like the professionals whom they nominally controlled, had been used to 'ruling the roost'. They did not always take kindly to being told what to do by the community or by professionals of low status who were only employed by a charity.

While much has been achieved over the twenty-two years since St Paul's was founded – parks have been designed and built where once there was rubble and dereliction, rows of attractive terraced houses which might have been bulldozed have been saved and renovated, decaying shopping areas have been given a face-lift, the priorities of the police have been adjusted to match those of residents – a very great deal remains to be done before it can be said that the area has moved far along the road from despair to recovery. However, what has become very clear, at least to St Paul's staff, is that just as they could not work as effectively as they would wish without also becoming involved in the process of community development, so also other specialists, whether architect, doctor, planner or politician, would also not be effective without similarly engaging with the wider community. The 'Building a Better Balsall Heath' campaign made fitful progress as attitudes changed before going into reverse every time one set of professionals was promoted away from the area to be replaced by a new one whose assumptions were more traditional.

IS ST PAUL'S SPECIAL?

In one sense there is nothing that is original about St Paul's for each town in the land can boast of several voluntary nurseries. Whilst the resource centre is elaborate there are many adventure playgrounds, especially in the inner areas. In recent years the number of city farms has grown. Quite a number of community newspapers have been formed. Certainly many areas celebrate with a carnival or a bonfire night.

Perhaps what is distinct about St Paul's is that it organizes all these activities, boasts a school and more besides. Its functions cluster within one community servicing and supporting the dozen local schools within the area and the community itself. They form an integrated community education and development project which is also independently managed by representatives from the community. St Paul's has gone further than most in rekindling a variety of educational and social insititutions within which local people can find and develop an identity. It has restored something of the warp and weft of the community which had become so frayed and tattered that it could not hold people securely within its social fabric.

Birmingham can boast of two other outstanding voluntary organizations to add to its many smaller ones. When St Peter's teacher training college in Saltley became empty, it was bought by a local trust and now houses a wide range of local enterprises and devolved parts of city departments. It has come to resemble a kind of mini town hall. The Birmingham Settlement in Newtown was established many years ago. It now provides a wide range of local economic, social and training facilities and has had

a substantial impact on the neighbourhood. Most towns can now point to one or more community development enterprises like these which play an important part in kindling the spirit of their area. Yet they remain the exception rather than the rule and they face many uphill battles.

So, before a false impression is given, it must also be reported that while Balsall Heath has halted the cycle of decay and begun to reconstruct its community, a great deal of work remains to be done. Further, it cannot be claimed that its bottom-up efforts have become securely grafted on to a responsive top-down equivalent. The relationship is a difficult one. Too many in the community still resent central authority and feel that it does not understand or sympathize with its needs. Too many in the city feel threatened by the community's attempts to manage its own affairs and react with hostility born of defensiveness. It is most important to remedy these defects if the process of revitalization is to be speeded. There is much work still to be done, yet there is a model here which is worthy of replication in many other inner and outer city areas. How might this be achieved?

REFERENCES

Hart, V. (1992) *Balsall Heath, a History*. Studley: Brewin Books.
Heathcote, D. (1992) *Language Alive!* Birmingham: St Paul's.

Chapter 5

From the Particular to the General Solution

Unlike most educational establishments, St Paul's was never within the state system of educational and social provision. As with countless other local charities this brought with it the tradition of low funding; the expectation that volunteers would provide key parts of the service for love rather than money; that students would fill in the gaps; that staff would work for less than statutory wages and that the agency was not an essential part of the system but occupied a subsidiary category for a few who did not qualify for or merit support from the superior provision of the State.

Yet charitable status and independence had clear benefits, including the vital ingredient of success. Visitors from other parts of the country asked: 'How can St Paul's be used as a model from which we can benefit?' Until recently, the answer had to be: 'With difficulty'. For, though cheap at the price, St Paul's as a whole had come to cost around £500,000 a year.

It would be idle to suppose that some city or state benefactor would provide each urban community with the extra finance necessary to help it to reproduce its equivalent of St Paul's. Indeed, it would be very doubtful that such extra provision on top of everything which already exists would be of any great value even if it could be afforded. For, at the heart of the St Paul's message is the belief that existing attitudes and styles of organization lie at the root of the urban malaise. Thus, any solution will not depend upon the simple reproduction of the form of St Paul's but on the application of its substance. It will entail the reconstruction of the attitudes and methods of existing organizations.

For many years, therefore, it seemed as if the project had become stuck in an impossible dilemma. It had proved its worth and people wanted it, but the funding and will necessary to duplicate it elsewhere seemed to be an insuperable problem unless the city could be persuaded to use its mainstream budgets differently. This had, of course, been the original idea behind the central government's investment in urban aid and ICPP. However, the understandable disinclination of the town hall to dismember and redistribute itself out to communities prevailed, for it felt it still had to provide services and schools for communities and that St Paul's was the exception which proved the rule rather than an experiment which showed why existing rules had to be changed. Little

could be done unless national factors caused enough pressure to build up to show that the radical reform of town hall provision had become essential.

Six nationally significant factors which had not until recently coexisted are of interest, for they have combined in a way which made reform unavoidable. The first concerns a simple organizational truth about how communities can be best helped, the second and third concern different aspects of the nation's economy, the fourth relates to the demands of an increasing number of parents, the fifth is revealed by the latest research about the power of schools to influence the progress of their pupils and the sixth is to do with the readiness of the political parties to accept the need for radical change.

THE ORGANIZATION OF COMMUNITY DEVELOPMENT

Erich Schumacher worked for the Coal Board in Britain. He developed the idea of intermediate technology for Third World aid programmes. His ideas, which were most clearly put in his book *Small is Beautiful* (1974), are of vital relevance to the urban areas of this country.

He wrote:

> The best aid to give is intellectual aid, a gift of useful knowledge. There are many reasons for this. Nothing becomes truly 'one's own' except on the basis of some genuine effort or sacrifice. A gift of material goods can be appropriated by the recipient without effort or sacrifice; it therefore rarely becomes 'his own' and is all too frequently and easily treated as a mere windfall. A gift of intellectual goods, a gift of knowledge, is a very different matter. Without a genuine effort of appropriation on the part of the recipient there is no gift. To appropriate the gift and make it one's own is the same thing ... The gift of material goods makes people dependent, but the gift of knowledge makes them free ... The gift of knowledge also has far more lasting effects and is far more closely relevant to the concept of 'development'. Give a man a fish, as the saying goes, and you are helping him a little bit for a very short while; teach him the art of fishing, and he can help himself all his life. On a higher level; supply him with fishing tackle; this will cost you a good deal of money, and the result remains doubtful; but even if fruitful, the man's continuing livelihood will still be dependent upon you for replacements. But teach him to make his own fishing tackle and you have helped him to become not only self-supporting, but also self-reliant and independent ... This approach, incidentally, also has the advantage of being relatively cheap, that is to say, of making money go a long way. For £100 you may be able to equip one man with certain means of production; but for the same money you may well be able to teach a hundred men to equip themselves.
> (p. 165)

It is quite clear that attempts to help communities to become revitalized, no matter how well-funded and well-intentioned, will fail if they do not involve people within these communities. This involvement will be of no avail if it takes only a token form. Success depends on key elements from within the community being in the driving seat, setting the agenda and taking a direct part in the redevelopment process. It is now understood that this principle applies whether the subject is the Third World or the inner and outer ring communities of Britain's own cities.

THE ECONOMIC EFFECT

In feudal times only the priest and scholar needed to be educated, while the large majority of the population could remain illiterate. An agricultural economy could happily sustain itself with the help of such an unequal educational system because the skills and knowledge needed for most farming and related craft jobs could be passed on by parental tradition and apprenticeships. There was no need for book-learning or deliberately organized intellectual skills in the workplace, home or community.

When the economic base of the UK shifted throughout the nineteenth century from dependence on farming and the countryside to being fashioned by industry and the rapidly growing town, then pressure built up for a literate workforce and a basic education for all. This demand resulted in the *ad hoc* development of an inferior kind of education for the previously illiterate 80 per cent of the population.

The flawed and inadequate education system which sustains so many underperforming schools and produces so many underachieving pupils requires drastic, radical change if it is to serve the new post-industrial needs of the nation. The economic circumstances now exist which make such change almost irresistible, for unlike in the manufacturing revolution of the nineteenth century, the information and technological revolution of today and the nation's prospects for the future do not demand a proportion of 20 per cent of the population who can lead and manage the remaining 80 per cent, who can be safely left to become the horny-handed workers. Rather, it now needs a workforce which is 100 per cent intelligent, articulate, capable of adjusting to rapid change and acquiring new skills several times within the span of a working life. Either the nation develops a world-class education system which nurtures the talents of all its children to the full, or it will be driven out of business by its competitors.

It became respectable to ask if the nation's schools are a factor in its economic decline. Labour's James (now Lord) Callaghan called for a great debate about education in 1976. Sir Keith Joseph and his successors have begun to tackle the problem which he exposed.

The boom years have faded. Times of scarce money have arisen. These are compounded by the ever-increasing cost of health care, care for the elderly, education, welfare benefits, social services and other aspects of the welfare state. How can publicly funded agencies now be afforded? Are there fresh ways of using existing money which can make it go further? Can private agencies play a part in the provision of publicly agreed components of the welfare state? Can voluntary effort be mobilized? Can parts of what used to be state provision be run as separate, cost-effective, independent centres? Necessity is the mother of invention. So, in times of finite funds and growing costs, new approaches are forced on to the agenda.

During the 1980s a Labour administration in New Zealand was the first to respond with imagination to its economic difficulties. It devolved large portions of its previously centralized welfare state out to the regions and to autonomous agencies. A number of western nations have begun to follow suit, not always in a systematic way. In the United States of America, some states have responded more rapidly than others. In Britain, some government departments and some town halls have begun to grasp the nettle more firmly than others. Initially, such action was taken for negative, defensive reasons – how can we spend less and save more? There could and should be positive, pro-active reasons – how can we deliver better, more cost-effective services to people in communities by helping them to help themselves?

THE PARENTAL EFFECT

The concerns of parents and communities now coincide with the dawning economic need for swift, radical reform. Yesterday, the parents of the failing 80 per cent knew that their children would still find gainful, if unenviable, work. They could afford to say to their children: 'School never did me any good. It's unreal. You endure it until you can leave and enter the real world which we know about. Just keep your nose clean until you follow your father into the factory or down the mine'. Today, parents know that they must convey a different message. For, without an educational ticket of introduction to the world of work their child may never find employment or gain the security necessary to raise a family and find purpose and meaning in life. Some parents do not necessarily know how to help their child, for their own experience remains one of failure. They may sometimes lack confidence, but every parent is fiercely concerned for their child's future and will do what they can to influence it positively.

It is not easy for the professional parent, who is better equipped to influence the 'system' and find a place at one of the good schools, to know quite what it is like for other parents whose children face failure in the future because they have absolutely no alternative but to attend the 'bad school down the road'. Just recall how certain the prospects are for the 80 per cent or, in Birmingham's case, the 83.3 per cent. These statistics of failure spell personal disaster for the child and the family. It marks them in their attitudes and prospects of work and security for life and because, today, this very private and personal tragedy also spells economic disaster for the city and the nation, the once quiet and unconfident voice of the parent can now be heard. As the months go by it is likely that this voice will get louder and louder until all are forced to take notice and act to remedy the situation.

THE SCHOOL EFFECT

The biblical saying 'faith can move mountains' finds a modern expression in the Hawthorne effect. Psychologists demonstrated scientifically what most people know by instinct, namely that people achieve significantly better results if they are led to believe that they can do so. For many years no one believed that it was possible to run a mile in under four minutes. Since Roger Bannister proved that it was possible, the four-minute barrier is now broken as a daily routine. Because St Paul's school staff persuade their errant pupils that they can and will succeed, they do so. Because a group of unconfident people are told by 'experts' that achieving a particular task is confidently expected of them, then they are able to accomplish it.

Suprisingly, generations of educationalists and politicians, though not parents, believed that a school had little effect upon the educational performance of a child. Because the comprehensive school had 'failed' to narrow the educational and social distinctions between the 20 per cent and the 80 per cent they thought that they had found evidence that schools merely confirm the ability which the child 'brings' to school from home.

In a profoundly important book, *The School Effect* (1989), David Smith and Sally Tomlinson recently showed that research which focused on the ability of schools as instruments of social engineering to narrow the differences between individuals and

groups, so making them more equal, had diverted attention from their ability to either boost or hold back the performance of children at all levels of attainment. Following Rutter's (1979) pathfinding study, *Fifteen Thousand Hours* (the number of hours which the normal child spends at school), they demonstrated that the performance of apparently similar urban schools was in fact widely different, and that a child who went to a poor school would not do as well as one who went to a good one. 'The result of going to an effective school can be seen as an increment on the performance of each child that goes to it. This increment may be large enough to be very important for its effect on what each individual is actually capable of doing.'

Smith and Tomlinson pointed out that many educationalists have not been as concerned with scholastic performance as with other, less measurable, social aspects of education. These educationalists have argued that:

> . . . children in the schools that achieve badly in scholastic terms might be receiving other benefits. Today, that argument seems far-fetched. The various objectives of education are all related to the central enterprise of acquiring skills and knowledge. Schools are hardly likely to achieve the various related objectives by ignoring the central one. Children who are ignorant, poor at reasoning and unable to express themselves clearly are unlikely to be creative, constructive, spiritual or good at team work.

It seems likely, they say:

> that poor scholastic achievement is accompanied by further disadvantages. Hence, we find . . . that children who make good progress in scholastic terms also tend to participate in a range of school activities outside the classroom . . . In any case, it is a matter of common observation that the schools with high academic standards . . . are ones that also offer a broad curriculum and a wide range of activities outside the curriculum.
> (p. 302)

Parents have always known what Smith and Tomlinson pointed out in clear statistical terms. That is why those who can afford to do so send their children to the best public schools and those who cannot will, if they are able to do so, move house or even town so as to be near to a good state school. People began to ask: 'Why should we have to do this? Why can't we influence the school round the corner so that it becomes good and attractive?'

It is now quite clear that good schools are not defined by whether they fit into the public or grammar school category. Nor are they, therefore, restricted in number, for any school serving any area can be transformed into a good school provided that the will, vision and dedication are there. Professor Tim Brighouse made the point that an underachieving school can be transformed in a three- to four-year period if key factors are present and if the personnel are determined enough. 'Where there is a will there is a way.' This suggests that the educational performance of the children and schools of a whole town and, indeed, the whole nation could be transformed in a surprisingly short period of time to the satisfaction of the economy and the parents as well as the teachers. But what is the way? And where is the will?

THE POLITICAL PARTIES

It is not surprising that the performance of schools has recently worked its way to the top of the agenda of all the political parties. They all now accept the need for

communities to develop and become revitalized. The economic needs of the nation can not be ignored as competitor countries head the growth tables. Votes and electoral success are tied to economic success as well as to the demands of parents. Further, it is now difficult for politicians to escape the implications of research on the effects of good schools on their pupils. Until recently, however, politicians have not been united about how to put matters right. Indeed, for a long time they have been heatedly opposed to each other on key matters and uncertain and confused on others. They have, therefore, unintentionally stood in the way of the radical reform of the educational system by asking the wrong questions about the wrong issues and so causing thinking on the subject to be muddled.

On the one hand, as if by theoretical instinct, Labour has wished to abolish the public and grammar schools. Its policy has been to 'nationalize' and to unify education, thus sending all children to the same kind of state comprehensive school. Because these state schools are 'enriched' by the presence of 'the most able' children in a non-selective system, the theory goes, then standards will be automatically raised and a new social equality created. Labour theorists have been able to justify the fact that most schools continued to underachieve because 'bright' children have been 'creamed off' by the best independent and grammar schools. They continue to tilt at the public and grammar schools as the cause of the malaise. They have thus managed to avoid asking why so many state schools are not good while others are excellent and so they also avoid searching for other remedies which would be triggered by the question: how can all state schools be improved in their own right? On the other hand, the theoretical instinct of the Conservatives has in the past led them to support the schools of the affluent and the wealth creators whilst also preserving and developing the state system because of the prevailing cultural consensus for the welfare state.

Most recently Labour has charged the Conservatives with trying to 'privatize' the best state schools, while ignoring the needs of the others, while the Conservatives accused Labour of wanting to destroy the best schools for dogmatic egalitarian reasons which were unrelated to the real world. As time passed, however, these traditional Labour and Conservative arguments began to founder on the rocks of urban blight, economic reality, the school effect and parental concern. Both the main political parties have belatedly begun to seriously address the age-old question: how can the performance of all schools be raised to the level of the best so that all children are able to develop to their full potential both educationally and economically? This represents a most important step forward.

Although the Conservative Governments of the 1980s and early 1990s may have arrived by a different route at the same conclusion as Erich Schumacher, they began to apply it in their health, housing, social and educational policies. In a speech just before the 1992 general election Douglas Hurd wrote: 'The only way to meet human needs is to empower citizens, decentralize decision-making, and shift the balance towards the users of services, both by strengthening their rights and by boosting the responsibility of the professionals who serve them.'

In the case of education, this entailed diminishing the significance of the local education authorities, even their dissolution, and the transfer of most, if not all, education funds and control to schools. All schools now have the potential to become self-governing state schools by the turn of the century. The economic, cultural, financial and political climate in which St Paul's was born twenty-two years ago has changed

completely. In the early days it often seemed as if it was swimming against the tide of events. Along with other charities it was a peripheral and insignificant phenomenon. Now that tide has turned. Every school could occupy a similar status and, as we shall see, because each school could regain the whole of its budget from the town hall, the possibility arises for duplicating a variety of the local community services which St Paul's offers.

REFERENCES

Rutter, M. et al. (1979) *Fifteen Thousand Hours*. Wells: Open Books.
Schumacher, E. (1974) *Small Is Beautiful*. London: Abacus.
Smith, D. and Tomlinson, S. (1989) *The School Effect*. London: Policy Studies Institute.

Chapter 6

The End of Town Hall LEAs

A host of pioneers festoon the early days of the state system of schools for all. The schools they built, financed, staffed, supervised and led were heroic achievements. Since those times, the Industrial Revolution which created the backcloth for these profound educational developments, has been superseded. The population of towns has grown apace and the economic and educational needs of the country have changed substantially.

Towns are now huge, multifaceted urban sprawls with a thousand different interests and neighbourhoods. For example, by 1991 Birmingham's LEA (which is not, as some think, the largest in Britain) administered, managed and financed over 400 schools, their buildings, the 170,000 pupils who attended them, the 10,000 teachers and the 11,000 ancillary staff who support the teachers with caretaking, school-meal and other duties. In 1991 this city-wide industry cost over £400,000,000. It had become a huge concern. Today, the task of centrally administering such a 'system' has become dramatically different from the function of building new schools 100 years ago.

The longer this once admirable attempt to fashion a modern universal system based on town hall management is persisted with, the more it will creak, crack and fall apart at the seams in a series of spectacular failures. It is simply beyond the ability of ordinary human beings to administer such a system. The bureaucracy of the LEA which has built up over the years in a valiant attempt to do so has become a *Titanic*. Bereft of its founding vision, it is now impossible to steer as it heads for the iceberg of popular discontent with its product.

There is nothing new about a once-radical institution becoming outmoded with the passage of time. It happens to all institutions and there is no need to be ashamed or critical about this provided that we now accept and state clearly that if the once pioneering LEAs were businesses then they would be bankrupt before dawn broke tomorrow. They are locked into the needs of the industrial past and cannot respond to what the parents, schools and the new economy now require.

After decades of success in the industrial arena, ICI also became top-heavy and complacent, until its new chairman, John Harvey-Jones (1988), slimmed it down and turned it round. His subsequent role as a troubleshooter for ailing industries has become

renowned. Two management experts, Charles Handy, in *The Age of Unreason* (1989), and Valerie Stewart, in *The David Solution* (1990), have explained the simple, common-sense theory behind Harvey-Jones' achievements.

They point out that most organizations first go through a pioneering and innovatory stage. In this stage key people set the pace and aims for others. After a while, the very success of the organization creates the need for written rules and codes of conduct. These can grow until they overtake the original aims of the organization with the rules becoming ends in themselves. Head office, routines and bureaucracy can come to obliterate initiative and depress confidence and effort.

This can spell ruin for a business which lives or dies in a competitive world. In the case of a monopoly it can lead to a poor service which only survives because no one can muster the courage to overcome sentiment and switch off its life-support system. Very many businesses today have reached this harsh phase of their existence. Some of those who have competitors have not survived. Those which have survived have had to pain-fully transform themselves, often with the catalytic help of external experts like Harvey-Jones, Handy and Stewart.

The survivors are characterized by a determination to return to basics and recreate a sense of innovation and shared purpose. They are helped in this by what Valerie Stewart calls 'bureaucracy busting' and by what Charles Handy calls the move from the 'pyramid' style of top-heavy organization to the style of the 'maypole'. The head office of the maypole-like organization merely enables the many 'ribbon holders' and 'dancers', who were its dependent workforce, to co-ordinate their individual efforts by offering them exciting goals. The component parts of a once pyramid-like organization need no longer 'belong' to the same company. Each can be a separate, independent, DIY operation which links with others through common values and interdependent needs.

The values which drive the contrasting cultures of the pyramid and the maypole are significant. The rationale for the pyramid is derived from the organization. It is its own self-interested end. This is the hallmark of a producer, or supply-driven system. It is not committed to the community in which it is based and which it supplies with goods or services. It is this culture which led the president of General Motors to arrogantly assert, 'What's good for General Motors is good for America'.

The rationale for the maypole is quite different. It exists to serve aims beyond itself. It is consumer- and customer-driven. Of necessity it is committed to the community which surrounds it and which it serves. As if to echo President Kennedy it says, 'Ask not what your country can do for you, but what you can do for your country'.

How can these principles of good management and organization be applied to the educational arena? Driven by the need to raise standards and to improve the economic performance of the country, the Prime Minister, James Callaghan, started the great education debate in 1976, with the help of Shirley Williams. Before very long, how-ever, the economy and the winter of discontent ended his Government before he could provide answers. So it fell to the radical Conservative Governments of the 1980s to find a way forward. They agreed that each LEA had become complacent. Neither Conservative- nor Labour-controlled LEAs were providing schools and teachers with the support, targets or incentives they needed.

The Government's first bold reform called for a national curriculum to give all children and teachers high and clear aims. Schools were challenged to raise standards. They responded admirably but made the point that if they had no extra resources they

could not achieve the desired results. The problem did not lie with teachers – they worked hard and were dedicated to their children. Nor was the poor quality of LEA officers the cause – many were excellent. Rather, it lay in the long-standing organizational relationship between the pyramid-like LEAs and schools and communities. The control and management of education resided with the centralized LEAs while its practice and delivery were given to each individual school. The real consumers, parents and communities, were not even a part of the equation. This separation between control, management, practice and consumption gave an impossible task to both LEAs and teachers and no task at all to parents and communities, who had the greatest stake in the 'product', along with the nation.

The Government decided to replace the supply-led LEA management pyramid with a fresh system which had to respond to what the school and parents wanted, putting communities and schools, not the LEA, in the driving seat. The new system was to be customer- and demand-driven, not controlled by a single supplier which had no incentive to reform its practices.

So, the Government reformed the way schools were managed and financed. No one knew until recently that a primary school might cost as much as £700,000 annually and a secondary school £2,000,000 to maintain. The way each LEA had been organized meant that it did not see either the budget or needs of each individual school but only those for the totality of schools. For a very long time no school had ever seen any of the money which was spent on its behalf nor could it influence how it was spent. Therefore, the Government insisted that each LEA's funds and the responsibility for spending them should be given to schools, their teachers and elected governors. Every school now knows what its budget is. Since April 1993 it has also been supposed to have at least 85 per cent of that budget in its own hands.

This radical move to local management of schools (LMS) was intended to prepare the way for most, if not all, schools to gain the confidence to seek the full 100 per cent of their budget, by becoming autonomous, community-controlled, state grant-maintained (GM) schools. Table 6.1 shows what the reallocation of existing resources and GM status causes the typical primary and secondary school to gain over their LEA-controlled (LM) neighbour. Those which have become GM and control all their budget say that each school spends a third of this money on replacing the old LEA services with more effective ones, whilst the rest can be deployed as they choose at the chalk-face.

Table 6.1 *Typical annual budgets for LM and GM schools.*

Type of school	Typical budget if school is GM (£)	15% retained by LEA post-April 1993 if school is LM (£)	Typical budget if school is LM (£)
Primary	700,000	105,000	595,000
Secondary	2,000,000	300,000	1,700,000

These sums make GM status look inviting at first. However, they became less significant as LEAs felt obliged to devolve more and more of their once centrally retained budget out to individual schools in an attempt to minimize the attractive financial alternative of full independence.

However, finance is not the only or even the main reason for becoming GM. The most

compelling argument for autonomy lies in the fact that management and practice are brought together within each school. No longer can the budget be spent by remote officials on items which the school may not have chosen. Rather, it is spent by the school itself. Independence from the LEA means that each individual school gains the responsibility to manage and target its whole budget on the precise needs of its own classrooms. Each school becomes accountable not to the town hall but to parents and its catchment community via its elected governing body.

Devolution from an LEA does not create more money. It means that existing money can be deployed differently and put to the best possible use by the practitioner. This in turn generates fresh attitudes within the school and catchment community, creating a sense of ownership and control over buildings and resources. Instead of things being done to schools, schools can take charge of events and make things happen.

As Erich Schumacher recognized, independence creates self-respect and pride and so performance and standards are bound to rise. There is a profound organizational and cultural distinction between the old way of doing things, separating the central management of education from its practice in schools and the wishes of parents, and the new way, bringing together the three interrelated features of the educational process under the roof of each individual school. Compared with the existing unwieldy, pyramid-like monopoly of the LEA and the impotence of schools, independent maypole-like management and accountability to parents and the community are worth their educational weight in gold. For this reason the new autonomous schools are more accurately defined as self-governing (SG) rather than grant-maintained (GM) since GM merely refers to the way they are financed. Subsequent reference acknowledges this point by referring to such schools as SG ones.

Each LM school's new experience in managing 85 per cent or more of its budget shows what the school could do with 100 per cent of it. The schools which have already become SG report that the benefits are significant. However, what to parents spells excellence can evoke fear and resistance in the heart of the once all-powerful LEA because it is losing its century-old empire. The reforms which benefit children, release energy and raise the expectations of the school are against the interests and *raison d'etre* of the existing LEA.

Schools and the LEAs each face a choice. Schools must ask: can we run our school better than the LEA? If left to their own devices most would choose self-government. They might hesitate, because of a lingering loyalty to the collectivist culture of central planning, but they will be tempted to put their children and the ability to do their job first.

The choice for an LEA is very different. Some LEAs are deciding to help their schools to gain SG status which is enlightened self-interest. The LEA could survive in radically changed form if it created the maypole-like context in which schools could thrive as autonomous agencies. However, other LEAs, both Conservative- and Labour-controlled, are choosing a different approach. They are using the dated, pyramid-like culture of central planning to slow the move to SG in an attempt to retain their authority. What will happen? Will schools become SG in significant numbers? Will most LEAs help them to do so? Or, will they try to halt the process and perhaps inject conflict into what otherwise might have been a gradual move from LM to SG, from the pyramid to the maypole organization?

THE TWO CULTURES AND LANGUAGES OF DEPENDENCE AND AUTONOMY

Schools have been locked into an unquestioned relationship of dependence upon their LEA for generations. It is not just the formal power and authority which LEAs have over schools which holds them in its embrace. State schools have known no alternative to the culture of collectivism and central planning which provides the rationale for the existing way of organizing the state system of education.

The long-standing culture of dependence tells schools that there is something essentially good about the town hall's central management of their 'family' of schools. Collectivist, left-wing arguments sound 'instinctively' better than individualistic right-wing ones because they coincide with the security which the status quo offers and reflect the only experience of 'care and co-operation' which schools have ever known.

Schools may grumble about the poor services which the LEA monopoly supplier has given them, but they prefer 'the devil they know' to uncertainty and the fear of the unknown. Schools cannot easily see the virtues of the SG alternative because they have not been told where it is leading. They also find it difficult to disentangle the case for autonomy from Tory dogma about 'privatization and the market place'.

It is now clear that the Conservative architects of the 1988 legislation did not understand how deeply entrenched the pyramid-like 'system' had become. They wrongly supposed that once state schools were formally free to opt out of the state monopoly then they would immediately clamour to become state independent schools in the same way that a nationalized corner shop might relish the chance of privatization – not so much a maypole, more a free-for-all.

In fact, schools which contemplate SG feel exposed and vulnerable. Thus, a school which is tempted by independence is easily persuaded that this is analogous to being seduced into a furtive extramarital affair by the goddess of the marketplace. The rejected culture and institutions of the LEA 'family' pull out all the moral stops to shame the school into staying. They accuse it of greed, individuality and lack of care for its neighbours. Schools feel guilty. The tactics of fear which some LEAs use to bully schools into submission are hardly necessary as guilt and conscience can be more persuasive than brute force.

This analogy sees LM and SG as polar opposites. LM is cast as good, SG as bad. So the choice of SG inevitably leads to cultural condemnation, tears, conflict and divorce from the family. Although it is the culture of dependence and its institutions which have imposed this destructive definition on to the situation and resisted Harvey-Jones type entreaties to move with the times, it is the school which is accused and blamed. Both the would-be SG school and the organizational case for autonomy can, therefore, be wrong-footed by a powerful inherited culture and language which identifies SG with a Conservative Government and unfettered individualism.

This may be understandable, but it is not inevitable or reasonable. In addition to modern organizational theory, there is also a radical traditional culture and language in Britain which reveres the individual and which legitimizes self-control and independence within the common good. The Chartists and the founders of the Labour Party used this tradition to argue their case against the injustice and inefficiency of the uncaring autocratic state of the last century. Perhaps it is time to resurrect this tradition and show that in tandem with modern organization theory it provides at least as firm

a basis for justifying the local control of schools by communities as socially questionable Conservative theories about market forces.

The alternative radical analogy to 'SG equals divorce' suggests that a school which considers SG should be seen more as a dependent child growing up, seeking the key to the door and gaining an independent maturity. The LEA parent who does not assist the child to assume its right to become independent, who seeks to delay the process or reverse it, is cast as possessive, jealous and dictatorial and a bad manager.

This analogy sees LM and SG not as opposites but as occupying different points on a continuum, with LM representing adolescence and SG the point of full maturity for which all schools should aim. It also suggests that wise LEAs should not resist but actively help schools to move in this direction and to develop a new generation with new needs of its own and new ways of answering those needs. This model sees both LM and SG as being good. SG is merely a more advanced state of maturity than LM.

If the analogy of 'growing up' is to be successfully asserted against that of 'divorce', then schools also need to be offered a convincing 'vision' of how LM does lead naturally to SG, of how to replace the last generation's dated institutions of dependence with the vigorous new ones which are necessary to sustain a dialogue between an adult association of equals.

It seems that there are two possible ways in which the Government's reforms might develop, one regressive, the other progressive.

THE REGRESSIVE OR CONFLICT MODEL – LM AND SG AS OPPOSITES

Although introduced by a Conservative Government and, thus, at first opposed by the left, LM can be seen as a way of preserving the ageing LEA, while SG can be seen as Conservative and opposed by many on the left because it will lead either to the radical change or dissolution of the once caring LEA.

At first, only some schools will dare to go SG. Conflict will be injected into the situation as LEAs defend the status quo and prevent more schools from following in their wake. A two-tier system could arise in which an LEA marshalls LM schools on its side of a self-inflicted divide, while SG schools are forced to occupy the other side and to risk overidentification with the policies of a Conservative Government.

The LEA risks becoming the repository of the poor, less ambitious schools, while SG schools become identified with independence and success. LEAs could become more and more embitttered. Both the political and local versus central government conflict could get worse. Political dogma could become even more strident and the period ahead could become uncomfortable and strained. The age-old, economically damaging, 20:80 split between schools for a past-industrial elite and schools for the masses could persist, and the needs of post-industrial society could be denied – at least for a while.

In an attempt to preserve the once reforming LEA, it seems that many on the left could inadvertently introduce conflict and make it more likely that LEAs will struggle to survive before going out of business rather than adjust to new times and prosper. Equally, the Government must bear part of the blame. It failed to present the move to SG as a neutral organizational device and underestimated the negative way in which LEAs and the left would respond to their reforms. It did not paint a clear or constructive enough path which they expected the reforms to take.

THE PROGRESSIVE OR HARMONIOUS MODEL
– LM AND SG AS A CONTINUUM

The conflict model forces schools to choose once and for all between a pyramid-like (LM) and a rival, maypole-like (SG) camp, but it seems more sensible to see the choice in different terms. It is possible to choose LM for an initial period before going on to choose SG at a later stage. The choice of LM could last for months or years while a school gains the experience and confidence to wean itself from the LEA and opt for independence. Schools could and should be given unpressured time by an enlightened LEA before being helped by it to move from one point on the continuum to another.

While schools are helped by LEAs to move gradually from LM to SG, LEAs themselves could gradually dismantle their pyramid-like organizations. This phased process of transition would allow the city fathers time to construct a bright new role for the town halls as enablers and facilitators of self-governing state schools and of their catchment communities.

The scenario of the harmonious model is a valuable one and quite unlike that of the conflict model (see Figure 6.1). Once the first schools have become SG this scenario entails an educational John Harvey-Jones persuading LEAs that it is best to move with the times and voluntarily give schools more and more of their budgets until the full 100 per cent of the finance available for education has been devolved. As this point is reached a wise town hall will have anticipated the need to close its LEA down and replace it with a new department which is relevant to the needs of the newly independent state schools. This will enable town halls to modernize themselves and carry a fresh torch for local democracy.

Once this harmonious transition is underway it is no longer necessary for each individual school to separately go through the process of becoming SG and risk conflict, tension and the creation of a two-tier system. For their enlightened LEA will, in effect, have helped all schools in its area to become independent. The parent vote required to take the final step could become a formality, while remaining symbolically most important. There are many advantages in this route to independence.

- Schools are not pressed into taking an either/or choice, but can move along a continuum at their own pace towards independence with the help of their LEA.
- The culture of the pyramid and dependence is replaced by harmony and the culture of the maypole and independence.
- The transition is supported by the LEA and town hall, so conflict between different types of school and a two-tier system are avoided.
- Political stances are avoided. Independence for schools and the need for an entirely new kind of support from the town hall can be worked out and accepted on organizational merit alone.
- The LEA undergoes a vital, phased and agreed constructive change as it moves from a pyramid-like organization to a maypole-like one. First, LEAs as we have known them really do cease to have a meaningful function and disappear. Second, this represents no more of an attack on local government than John Harvey-Jones' attempts to rescue fading businesses by radical reorganization signifies an attack upon them. Thus, conflict between local authority town halls and central government can be avoided. Third, councillors and town halls are freed from the impossible

task of managing and financing all the schools in their area. This gives the town hall an opportunity to replace dated, irrelevant departments with a reduced number of new 'interdepartmental' departments. For example, in future a single department could encompass the functions of the traditional social services, recreation and leisure, and education departments. The role of the new-style department is no longer that of provider but one of enabler to a variety of community-based independent agencies of which schools are only one example. The various possible models of a local educational system from the pre-existing one through LM and SG to fully SG are illustrated in Figure 6.1.

Staffordshire and other authorities are in the process of delegating the full 100 per cent of their budget to schools. Kent, Hillingdon and other authorities are setting up new children's and community departments in place of their existing LEA and other departments. Both the councillors' and the town halls' finance, effort and offices are freed from the impossible tasks of crisis management. They could become the visionary facilitators of an urban Renaissance.

Town halls are already devolving more and more of their traditional functions to communities. Forced by the constraint of economic necessity, they no longer wish to control top-heavy traditional, specialist departments. They are introducing more up-to-date ones which recognize as discrete entities the many rural and urban villages which make up each area and town. So far they have done this out of a sense of adversity and a struggle for survival but the time has come to avoid reacting to circumstances, to seize the initiative and set a positive lead.

Charles Handy points out that most modern business practices 'increasingly find that they can most usefully . . . identify the essential core of their task and leave the rest' to the initiative of others. This is the likely future role for both central and local government and political parties as well as business organizations.

Now that the first state schools to become self-governing are enjoying the pride and exhilaration of independence which St Paul's initially experienced more than twenty years ago, it is important to look at them in detail. They may well state the case for independence more eloquently than a theory of organization.

Once the virtues of the school have been explored it will be possible to return to discuss in greater detail the exciting opportunities which they open up for town halls and the practice of local democracy. It may be that when those who are currently attracted to the conflict model can see the benefits for pupils and teachers, and the radical implications of the new schools for economic and urban development, then they can be persuaded to opt for the harmonious way forward.

REFERENCES

Handy, C. (1989) *The Age of Unreason*. London: Hutchinson.
Harvey-Jones, J. (1988) *Making It Happen*. London: Fontana.
Stewart, V. (1990) *The David Solution*. Aldershot: Gower.

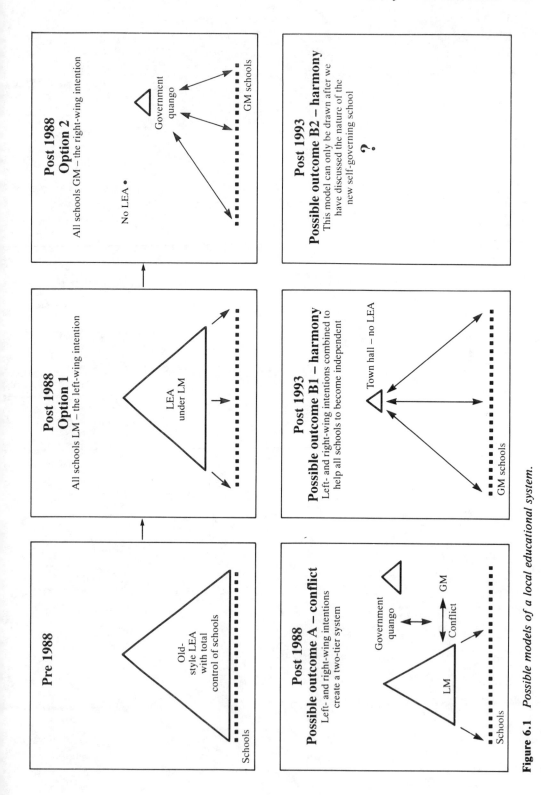

Figure 6.1 *Possible models of a local educational system.*

Part 2

The New Self-governing Neighbourhood School

The legislation which enabled schools to govern themselves was approved by Parliament in 1988. However, four years later only 300 schools had chosen this option. These first schools were reviewed by Brent Davies and Lesley Anderson in 1992. Clearly some of these schools were more like grammar schools than typical state urban ones. Equally clearly, the Government had yet to make a convincing case for its policy since by the summer of 1993 only 600 schools had become SG. Even when 1,000 are SG (by late 1993) this will mean that only 4 per cent of Britain's 24,000 schools have chosen autonomy.

If self-government is to be made attractive to the remaining 96 per cent then the case for it must be spelled out in compelling detail. This detail must illustrate how the typical urban self-governing school will function, and that SG is not a politically biased option but one which is clearly in the interests of pupils and parents as well as teachers. The four chapters of this part of the book show what the politically neutral self-governing school might look like, the nature of its curriculum, the style of its teachers and its relations with its neighbours. Part 3 will then return to the discussion of how this school will relate both to the town hall and to its catchment community before considering the delivery of services to communities in post-industrial society.

REFERENCE

Davies, B. and Anderson, L. (1992) *Opting for Self-management*. London: Routledge.

Chapter 7

Signposts of Success

In the past when parents realized that existing schools were no longer relevant to their needs and hopes for their children, they usually found ways of creating new schools. The dissenting academies were built by the new, non-conformist industrialists because they believed that the medieval grammar school was not relevant to the dawning modern age. Later, the old grammar schools were saved from oblivion and some of them became the public or fee-paying independent schools of today. The elementary school was built as a result of pressure from the Labour movement for children who otherwise would have received no formal schooling.

Do we stand at a point where some new kind of school is beginning to emerge as a result of popular unrest with existing state schools? It is most likely, for parental and senior teacher pressure can now make itself felt on locally elected school governing bodies which have real influence over a school's policy. The school will further feel the pressure of parent or customer choice if the parents don't like the goods on offer, as they will shop elsewhere and the school will risk closure. Previously the LEA provided the state school for the community irrespective of its wishes. Because the school did not belong to the teachers or governors, they did not have to care if its appearance and standards were drab and low for blame lay elsewhere, with remote authority. The school knew it would still be there tomorrow whether its product was appreciated locally or not.

The new independent management of schools has transformed that situation. This school's future now clearly lies in the hands of the head and governors. The sense of responsibility and ownership which this gives to the staff and governors will become most important for the future of schools. It is good that they now know that their survival and the confidence of parents and the community lie in their hands. Their efforts – no one else's – will determine their school's reputation and continuation. By definition such schools will become the property and responsibility of their community. They will properly be called community schools. It is important to discuss in some detail the different features of the new school. These include the new educational culture and the organization of the new school.

THE NEW EDUCATIONAL CULTURE

Modern theory regards 'child-centred education' as the key to a good school's work. But a great deal of muddle-headed thinking surrounds the concept. Children do not know how they should be educated or what they should learn until they have gained stature, self-discipline and maturity. So, much of child-centred education has not been truly child centred at all but teacher centred. It has been derived from the theories and practices which they acquired from their universities and training colleges, places which have rarely encountered pupils like those who attend St Paul's. These have helped lead the way to permissiveness, pupil failure and that 'conspiracy of immaturity' of which an earlier chapter spoke.

If we are serious about focusing teaching upon the child, we risk making this error unless we recognize that 'child centered' necessarily means 'family centered' because it is the family of origin which consciously or otherwise provides the child with its early experience, views and values. Indeed, as the saying goes, 'give me a child for the first seven years and I'll give you the man'. What is learned, acquired and forged in these early years provides the skeleton or coat peg upon which hang the flesh, clothes, experience and values of later life.

If 'child-centred' education is really a shorthand way of describing 'family-centred' education, it is only a short step to realize that we must really speak of 'community-centred' education. In his or her early years, the child first begins to acquire human characteristics and his or her first perception of the world at his or her mother's breast. Before long, however, the father, if such there is, comes to play a role followed by others in what remains of the extended family. The family leads naturally on to other influences within the community and culture in which the child's developing life gains its meaning and *raison d'être*. Friends of the family become significant. So too does the atmosphere of the street, places of play and all the associations and connections which family and friends have with the outside world.

For these reasons, all education is child-, that is family-, that is community-centred. Good education has thus always been a shorthand way of talking about community-centred education or education in the context of family/community experience. But schools are not in themselves necessarily good things. Either by design or default, schools can enhance and supplement the informal, life-long educational process or they can hinder and confuse it. At its best, the education which a school offers takes the child's family and communal experience as its starting point. It uses it, stretches it, reflects on it and compares it with the experience of others to broaden horizons and sharpen skills. This leads to the special pursuits and tasks of later school years which help to place the young adult in the world of work and adult maturity with an ability to shape and take charge of his or her future.

Education which does not take the pupil's communally-derived experience and perception of what is relevant as a point of departure, or denies it, leads schooling to be seen as something foreign. School becomes a place to be endured until it can be left behind. After eleven years, the only certificate this school gives the school-leaver is one of failure. It is at loggerheads with the family and community. Not only the pupil, but also education and community suffer. The credibility gap widens and social tension increases.

For a school to be successful and its pupils to attain high standards, it follows that it must welcome and respect the pupil's family and community and engage with them

at the core of the educational process. In those instances where this does not happen naturally, the sensitive educationalist will ensure that the school and the home are pulling together in the same direction well before the child comes to school. Pre-school education will include those formal and informal measures which can be taken to heighten awareness of parenting skills. Every opportunity must be taken to underline the importance of language development and the acquisition of learning skills. Knowledge about and the use of health and related support services are important. The more pre-school parents come to see and use the advantages and opportunities of pre-school work, the playgroup, nursery and school itself, the more they will be able to help their child and the teacher when formal attendance is first required at reception class.

Many modern educationalists make the assumption that there is a distinction between 'school and formal education' on the one hand and 'society and informal education' on the other. At one level this can be true. We have just argued that when the school is bad, the separation between it and community becomes clear and distinct. Such a school is an imposition upon the natural educational process which takes place in the home and street.

When the school is good, it merely becomes a natural, interlinked, interdependent extension of the informal process of education in the community. In this sense, good education in school is merely formalized informal education. It is community education and the good school is necessarily a community school. The long-held tenet that a teacher merely acts *in loco parentis* is ignored at our peril.

It is not appropriate, therefore, to stress as some do, that community education is only about what goes on in pre-school work or in post-school, dual-use activities. This view can define community education as an 'optional extra' which can be 'bolted on' to the quite distinct 'real' educational process which takes place in school hours and within the classroom.

Even when the school's plant and facilities have been extensively used by the youth and community services there has often been little integration between host and guest. Typically, such schools have been selected secondaries with a wide, non-local catchment area because 'scarce resources' would not allow all schools to be so used. There has been a head of school and a quite separate head of centre. The remote LEA has financed and managed the school and either a different branch of the LEA or a different youth and community department has looked after the dual-use activities.

This organizational apartheid has been reinforced by conflicting educational and youth and community attitudes. The school has seen itself as serious and formal with evening use being seen as a hindrance. In turn, the youth and community warden's attitude is that the school is strict and austere while he or she is sympathetic to the community. Because school and community have tended to pull in opposite directions, even when the provision for both has been available in the same premises, the result has been confusion rather than mutual benefit. If school and community could be brought into mutually supportive, productive alignment then together they could boost standards and raise expectations in the school and community far more effectively than their separate contributions could do, particularly when these actually undermine each other.

It is not that either the school or community has the right approach and the other has the wrong one. Rather, the structure of the relationship between them both and the community they are supposed to serve has been ill-founded. However, the wisest

definition places community education at the very core of the educational process itself. It is *the* way of defining good education and cannot be distinguished from it. No school can function well and excite teachers and pupils unless the whole school becomes an extension of the life of the community and the community has a sense of ownership over and pride in its school.

The best education entails a full-blooded partnership between home, school and the community in which each plays a positive role which acknowledges and involves the others. Indeed, the national curriculum itself can only be brought to full and rich life by being seen as an integrated whole through the school's careful study of all aspects of life in the community. In turn, the good school will reflect, support and enhance the values and *raison d'être* of the social life in which it is situated.

For decades community educators have tried to capture what Henry Morris (1985) meant when he said that the best school lies 'athwart' its community and provides it, like the church or mosque, with a mirror which reflects its identity and a dynamo for assisting with its development. There have been many valiant attempts to achieve this aim and some exceptional successes. However, most of these have foundered on the fact that hitherto state schools have not belonged to their community. They are *in* it but not *of* it. They have been built and controlled by a distant town hall. There has always been a space, even a credibility gap, between them and their pupils and the community.

The new self-governing schools are independent of the town hall. They are accountable to parents and the community through their elected governors. This has transformed the situation, as an independent state school really can now be a part of its community because it is owned and controlled by it. Although the Government did not necessarily intend to create a situation in which every school could, quite literally, become a community school it has nonetheless done so. The point is well made by the parents of children who attend Small Heath School, which is situated in one of Birmingham's inner areas adjacent to St Paul's, and Baverstock School, which is in Druids Heath, the outer ring council housing estate to which many Balsall Heath families moved when their own homes suffered from slum clearance after the Second World War. In the mid-1980s, both Baverstock and Small Heath secondary schools were typical, depressing, off-the-peg, inner and outer ring urban comprehensives. They were suffering from falling roles, a singular lack of 'first choice' pupils and thus an unwilling clientele. Morale was low. Those Small Heath and Druids Heath parents who could afford to do so either moved or sent their children to 'better' schools in more 'prosperous' areas. So, in a losing battle to keep their numbers up both schools looked to families from way beyond their immediate neighbourhood.

These schools were suffering from the lingering death which threatens many such schools in many urban areas. Not long ago it seemed that both areas would eventually have no secondary school, thus further contributing to their decline and the decay of the city. However, since becoming self-governing, the parents and children have developed a fierce pride in both schools. For example, Baverstock parents defended their school vigorously at the time of the general and local elections of 1992. Had Labour won, the school would have been taken back into the control of the town hall.

'They said they'd take our school away. We couldn't let them do that. We won't let go,' said Mrs Humpage.

By way of explanation, the parents painted a bleak picture of the school when it was under LEA management and before it became independent. Mr O'Rourke said: 'You

should have seen the rotten windows and the roof. Every time it rained some rooms had to be closed and there were buckets everywhere. There wasn't much equipment. You felt nobody bothered.'

Mr Arris claimed that for many years the management of the building had been inadequate. 'It really was bad,' he said. 'After independence we got the resources to do the job. Staff turnover is down. We've got the stability, we've got a successful team now.'

'I used to be for the Council,' Mrs Pickerill said. 'But it doesn't work. I've come right round. We've only taken back what's ours by right. Now we've made something of the school, much more than they ever did.' Mrs Pickerill was angry with the Council. 'They really let us down. I felt badly about it at first. Now I think it's just better doing it our way.'

Mr Humpage agreed: 'It's something we never had before. Do you know, my kids can't wait for the holidays and weekends to finish. They love the place. They're doing really well, better than I ever did.'

Mrs Mills said: 'It's nothing to do with politics. It's about children. What they need, that's what's important. They've got it here. Every school should be like this if you ask me.' Everyone interviewed was very clear about this point. 'Maybe we did it first,' said Mrs Pickerill. 'But everyone should know how useful it is. They should all go for it.' Mrs O'Rourke had her grandchildren in mind when she argued that: 'It's got to be good for the little ones too. Every school needs what this one's got.'

Of course, most parents support the school which their children attend. There is nothing unexpected about Baverstock parents' positive views. It is the strength and depth of feeling which is unusual. Their enthusiasm for their children's school is almost tangible. This is special. The parents' vote of confidence must be an advantage for their children and a boon for staff. Many a head would be pleased to learn the formula which puts the light in the eye of Baverstock parents and which makes the school so much a part of the community.

The way these parents are thinking about how they and others can provide a good school for their children is also instructive. Their views have changed as they have experienced the benefits which their children have gained in the three years since the school went SG. They were clearly puzzled and hurt by Labour politicians who seemed not to be interested in the way they felt or what they had to say. This hurt turned to anger in the general and local elections. They voted for what they saw as the interests of their children against the opinions of their party.

As Mrs Humpage said: 'Why can't they put the children first before their own prejudices? We've proved we can make a better job of it than they ever could. Yet they've got the cheek to try to take it back. They'd ruin it again. I say to every school, you do it. You can have what we've got. If it's good for the kids it's got to be good.'
(*The Phoenix*, 1993)

Baverstock and Small Heath Schools really have closed the gap between themselves, the home and the community, ensuring that these three components of good education work in vibrant unison. There is no longer any danger that either school will close. They are both oversubscribed. Further, both schools opened sixth forms in 1993. Their communities were delighted and have received a real boost.

Community education is not simply another 'ism' or task which the already hard-pressed teacher must grapple with or, to gain peace of mind, postpone indefinitely. Rather, it is the only vision of education which makes coherent sense out of all the other reforms which schools face. It can turn a host of chores into an excitement of common purpose and excellent results.

THE ORGANIZATION OF THE NEW SCHOOL

Governors

Until recently the governing bodies of state schools were ineffective. They had no authority and no resources. The LEA was responsible both for the supply of education to the parent customers and for the quality of that education. However, the governors of SG schools are the key to this independence and the new-found accountability of schools to their customers. Governors, not the LEA, are now the SG school's final authority. They, not remote committees of councillors, set the policy guidelines for their school and assist with the major decisions which it has to take.

Once the school has become independent the governing body is made up as follows:

- Five parent governors who are elected by parents.
- One or two teachers who are elected by the teachers.
- The head teacher.
- At least one more first or foundation governor than the total of other governors. These governors are co-opted by the other governors, or church or founding authorities in the case of voluntary-aided church and other schools.

Becoming a governor is an important new form of community service. It enables each school to be owned and controlled by the community. It strengthens the community and returns to it buildings, employees and an educational process which for decades had been the province of remote civil servants.

The governors are like the directors of a company or community enterprise. They employ a managing director and staff to run the company's day-to-day affairs. However, they must help the head to judge whether the quality of the product is suited to the needs of the school's customers. They must oversee the school's development plan, its finances and the performance of staff and pupils. These are serious duties which are intended to guarantee that each school reflects and responds to the ambitions which parents have for their children.

The school development plan

Both LM and SG state schools have now become familiar with the idea of a development plan. Until recently, while under LEA management, school teachers tended to prepare separately each year's work and repeat it with little refinement the following year. The different aspects of the curriculum were not always co-ordinated and they did not develop in relation to coherent goals. Not only did the content of courses leave something to be desired but resources, rooms, buildings and grounds also did not play a significant part in the planning process. These vital aspects of the teaching process were divorced from the chalk-face of the school. They were left to the LEA to maintain. If such work was done at all, it took place in a haphazard manner. The few voluntary councillors who sat on the education committee had little hope of controlling the huge bureaucracy or helping it to plan carefully for the individual needs and development requirements of every school.

Once the Government had put the national curriculum in place, it made sense to ask each school to devise its own development plan and to regularly update it to meet changing circumstances and the exact needs of each individual school. Once stated, it is obvious that benefits will result if each school has to plan ahead to meet various objectives and to improve the range and quality of its teaching and the resources, buildings and grounds which form the context of the learning process.

Planning ahead, setting targets to cover developments over the next few years, and having control of the budget so that resources can be matched to curriculum needs does not answer every problem, but it can reduce crisis management and stress levels. More positively, it can help a school to improve the quality of its performance step by step and make it more accountable to the customer. It can give the whole staff a structured, mutually agreed means of focusing their individual and collective endeavours.

While there is no set formula for a development plan, each school will wish to include the following components:

- Curriculum.
- Personnel and staff development.
- Finance and resources.
- Grounds and buildings.
- Organization and management.
- Performance and results.
- Home/school/community.
- Marketing and promotions.
- Relations with other schools – there is scope for a cluster as well as a single school development plan.
- Governors.

When Hargreaves and Hopkins wrote their book *The Empowered School* in 1991, they could say in their chapter on 'Partnership between the LEA and schools' that 'most schools are at a relatively early stage in development planning ... and look to LEA officers to provide guidance and support'. Two years later in 1993 schools have become the experts in development planning as in a host of other matters such as the delivery of the national curriculum. They have left LEA officers and advisers behind. Indeed, too few LEAs yet have their own development plan, which is why both earlier and later chapters of this book suggest how local authorities can work out a way of catching up with all the implications of empowered and SG schools.

Those schools which read Chapter 12 of Hargreaves and Hopkins' book and feel that their LEA can still help and support them better than they can themselves are perhaps not yet ready to take the final step towards SG. However, those heads, chairs of governors and other key figures who can read that chapter and be convinced that there is nothing which their LEA can contribute which they could not improve upon themselves are surely ready to proceed apace towards full SG status.

As this point is reached of course, the school's existing development plan will need to be updated to include the initial steps to be taken. Then, upon a successful vote, the plan will again need updating to take in the responsibilities and advantages of SG status.

Hargreaves and Hopkins wrote their book to help schools to become more effective and to show that all children could achieve their potential. They conclude that:

For this to be achieved requires not simply better research, however practitioner friendly, but a profound change in school culture. Although few schools have yet achieved this cultural change, many are working on it. Where a school lacks the appropriate culture, development planning is a means of achieving it. The recognition by schools of this fact is the real and important condition of development planning. This is the key insight. If the school does so recognize, it will understand that development planning is not just about implementing innovation and change, but about changing its culture – or in more concrete terms, its management arrangements – to improve its *capacity* to manage (other) changes. (p. 123)

While each school needs its development plan to liberate its potential, it is but a short step for clusters of schools to develop a 'cluster development plan'. This point will be discussed in Chapter 10.

Performance indicators and quality control

The school's development plan will only be of value if the work of the school is regularly monitored with the help of a number of performance indicators. For example:

- How do the children fare at key stages in their development throughout their school life and not just in their SATs, GCSEs and A levels when their school life is at an end?
- What is the attendance rate – pupils and staff?
- What is the teacher–pupil ratio?
- When was the building last painted and the grounds weeded?
- Are teaching areas adequately equipped?
- What proportion of staff have been on courses in the last year?

The new school's inspection procedures were outlined in the Education (Schools) Act 1992. This act requires schools to give inspectors a variety of information gathered by performance indicators. This information is not just of interest to external inspectors. Far more importantly it will enable the school to evaluate its own work, ensure that the quality of its work is as high as it should be, that it has an accurate picture of its weaknesses and is clear about how these can be remedied and the development plan updated.

The production of 'league tables' from a common base such as SAT and GCSE results is attractive to the media and uninformed observers. Teachers and governors know that this could result in a school with advantaged children whose performance is not improving appearing far higher on the league table than a school with disadvantaged children whose results are rising sharply. For example, neither Baverstock nor Small Heath public exam results compare with those of Birmingham's grammar schools or those of LM schools in more affluent areas, but few schools are improving upon their own results at a faster rate.

Schools will, therefore, wish to produce their own graphs and tables which clearly show their 'value-added' factors to their customers and the wider public who otherwise might be denied a clear picture of how the school is performing. Any information which the school can gather about itself, its catchment community and the destiny of its pupils and staff will be of both internal and external use.

Data about a school's performance are only indications about the quality of that performance. The aim of performance indicators is to give assurances about the quality of a school's work to three categories of people.

- The governors and staff of the school, so that they can monitor strengths and weaknesses and constantly update their development plan.
- The parent–customers and the wider community, so that they can judge the quality of the service which is offered and choose between it and other establishments.
- The suppliers of funds to the school, so that they can have confidence in the fact that their finances are being well spent.

Parent–customers and the suppliers of finance to the school need the check of independent inspection to ensure that the school is kept on its toes. However, the real guarantee of quality will come from the school's own internal mechanisms for guaranteeing to itself that it is working in the way it wants and is meeting the targets which its own plan has set.

Some teachers and governors have been persuaded that quality assurance indicators such as SATs, development plans and a number of other reforms including independence have been distractions from the 'real' teaching process. They say: 'If only the teachers could be allowed to get on with their job everything would be alright'. Nothing is further from the truth. These developments make a coherent whole. So, indicators and quality assurance go right to the centre of the process of improving the quality of schools, raising standards and restoring confidence to what had become a discredited system.

A few facts and figures

By 1993, Baverstock and Small Heath Schools each had nearly four years' experience of autonomy, so it is useful to look at a few statistics provided by the schools to see how they have fared. Baverstock has a free school meal statistic of 30 per cent. Some 95 per cent of Small Heath's pupils are drawn from ethnic 'minorities'.

The number of parents who make these schools the first choice for their children has increased significantly. Whereas Baverstock used to draw its pupils from far and wide to make up its numbers, it now takes almost all its pupils from within a radius of a mile.

Table 7.1 *Parents' first choice.*

	1988	1992
Baverstock	243	550
Small Heath	151	247

Small Heath's results (GCSE grades A–C) have improved threefold and Baverstock's have doubled (see Table 7.2).

The attendance of pupils at both schools has improved, while truancy is almost non-existent, at a rate of 0.5 per cent at Baverstock and 1 per cent at Small Heath.

Table 7.2 *Examination results.*

	1988	1990	1991	1992
Baverstock	11%	13%	18%	23%
Small Heath	5%	9%	11%	17%

Table 7.3 *Pupil attendance (%).*

	1988	1992
Baverstock	87	96
Small Heath	86	93

Table 7.4 *Truancy (%).*

	1992
Baverstock	0.5
Small Heath	1.0

The number of pupils who stay in school for a midday meal has changed substantially. The number at Baverstock has tripled.

Table 7.5 *School meals.*

	Number of pupils		
	In the school	Staying in for midday meal	
		1989	1992
Baverstock	1170	330	997
Small Heath	867	362	509

Both schools have been able to add to the number of qualified staff through their use of the 15 per cent of their budget which would have been retained by the LEA had the schools remained LM.

Table 7.6 *Number of staff.*

	1989	1992
Baverstock	LEA numbers	+8.5 staff
Small Heath	LEA numbers	+6 staff

In 1989 the proportion of Baverstock parents who voted to become SG was 75.2 per cent of the total of 70 per cent who voted. In the summer of 1992 the BBC provided the funds for the vote to be held again. The parents who approved of SG were 99.34 per cent out of the total vote of 92.6 per cent.

Some vital services

1 *Insurance*. 'What happens if the autonomous school burns down?' 'What happens if lightning strikes or someone steals our computers?' Many governors and heads who ask such questions feel that the LEA can answer them positively while the independent option only offers uncertainty.

The Department for Education pays up to £6,000 of the costs of the comprehensive insurance of an SG school building, its staff, pupils and related contingencies. So the answer to the anxious questioner is: 'The insurance company of the school attends to the situation in the light of the agreement reached between it and the school.' It is likely that the school will insure far more items than the LEA and that an insurance company will act more speedily and efficiently than the LEA. After all, it needs the business and would like contracts with more and more schools. No doubt the school will shop around to get the best company and the best deal they can. Then, those who might otherwise have worried can rest easy.

2 *Supply teachers*. Many schools feel that their LEA has not provided a good cover teacher service. A desperate phone call about an emergency need for an infant teacher for Monday morning cannot be made to the LEA office until after 9.00 a.m. on the day the teacher is needed. Too often this resulted in a PE teacher arriving on Thursday, long after the crisis was over. Private agencies now exist which offer both LM and independent schools an around-the-clock instant and accurate response. Schools which use them say they have never had such a service and can't understand why no one ever thought of supplying it before. Insurance companies and supply teacher agencies show just how the 1988 education reforms have opened up the old LEA monopoly and enabled existing money to work in new, more effective ways.

3 *School meals*. The jokes about school meals – semolina and boiled carrots – stretch back for generations. While the old LEA service helped to feed many who otherwise might have gone hungry in the 1920s and 1930s, it had in recent times become lost up a culinary cul-de-sac. Those who should have been gaining a nourishing midday meal were going without. Both individual and school suffered because the 'chippy' down the road had driven a coach and four through what should have been a full and vital midday part of school life.

Private caterers have transformed this situation in SG state schools. In some schools there is 100 per cent attendance at the midday meal and a significant proportion arrive at 8.00 a.m. for breakfast. School life, as well as diet, has been given a real boost with a variety of exciting and tempting dishes. The price is right. Often, the old staff are kept on by the private contractor, so they were right also. Simply, it seems, the way they were managed and supervised was wrong. Competition, of course, has meant that the old LEA service has itself been forced to improve, just as its teacher supply service has shown signs of becoming 'customer friendly'. Whether it's a case of 'better late than never' or 'shutting the stable door after the horse has bolted' remains to be seen.

4 *Cleaning*. The new relationship which independent catering companies are developing with independent schools is also transforming school cleaning. It seems that an enterprising management and a contract concentrates the mind and the mop in equal

proportions. Again, it is often proving possible to retain existing staff and get from them a performance which is qualitatively different from the one a school had become accustomed to.

5 *Caretaking and administration*. Nicholas Chamberlaine is a secondary school in Warwickshire. The governors and head appointed a £20,000 a year 'professional administrator' who swiftly negotiated a new job description for the caretakers, which involved them in minor maintenance. They now have a workshop and portable work-bench, their job is more satisfying, their practical skills are used and valued, and there is a reduced need for outside contractors.

Administration and development

LM has already passed many of the functions of school management from the LEA to schools. The role of the head and senior colleagues has thus enlarged from that of leader and organizer of teachers to include the tasks of finance officer, computer operator, manager, administrator and servant of the governing body as well as deviser of development plans, insurance policies, etc. Yet, no additional staff have been allocated to help the head remain on top of this increased range of duties. This has led some to say: 'Teaching used to be fun. Now it's changed. I'm never in the class-room. Life is full of non-teaching chores and holds no pleasure.'

Some, therefore, suggest that the first post which a school contemplating SG should create is that of finance officer or bursar. This is not necessarily so. The head teacher and senior staff may find that a good administrator, manager or development officer is of much greater value to the school as well as a real relief to them personally. On reflection, schools may feel that a bursar is not necessary and that a book-keeper or part-time finance officer shared between a group of schools will suffice.

Independent fee-paying schools and free-standing colleges have had administrators and departments of administration for a long time. These leave the teachers and lecturers free to get on with the task of teaching and research. They also demonstrate that an LEA is not necessary for a school to survive and thrive.

In the past the LEA has performed the administration and management tasks for all state schools so these schools were dependent on the LEA. A primary school has been used to having only a part- or full-time secretary. A secondary school might have had two or three secretaries. Since LM, the head and senior staff have had to squeeze the roles of management and development between the vital tasks of teaching and leadership, making life very hectic. Important opportunities have been missed or indefinitely deferred.

If schools were used to having an administrator/development officer and thus were clear about the benefits of such a post, then they would probably all be queuing up to become SG. Indeed, as likely as not, the post holder would probably be leading the move to help the school to seize the benefits of independence. Because they do not have such a post and the vision and extra dimension of thinking which it brings to a school, many hard-pressed heads run the risk of having their eyes diverted from independence by all the other tasks which jostle for their attention and drag them reluc-tantly from the classroom.

LM offers to a school or group of schools the possibility of creating a post in advance of SG which can aid them with their development plans and the administration which such plans involve. The post holder could save the head and others much work and the stress entailed in preparing for independence and exploiting the benefits it offers.

A new officer would spare a head and senior staff from some of the burdens of timetabling, and a host of important paperwork chores. They would assist the new school with its own bids for capital finance, section 11 and INSET grants. They might deal with the contracts for school meals, caretaking and cleaning and with their supervision. They might help the school to pool some resources with its neighbours. Indeed, they might not only administer these resources but assist with their supervision. Their brief would be to help the head to target every available resource to the needs of the classroom and the school as a whole in conjunction with its neighbours.

Demonstrating excellence to the customer

The problem.   Following the 1988 Education Reform Act parents can and will shop around to find the right school for their child. This means that a school must not only be good and deliver what parents want but it must be seen to do so very openly and publicly. It must go out of its way to attract the customer.

This change is dramatic. Its importance for schools cannot be overemphasized. It builds a completely new dimension into the task of managing each school. It is no longer sufficient for a school to rest on the laurels of its record or for a school just to constantly strive to improve its performance. It must go out of its way to illustrate what it does to the widest possible audience of parents and opinion leaders in the community from which it seeks to recruit pupils.

The image which LEA schools can signal to parents is: 'State school – second best. Try elsewhere first.' Many parents do just this.

In the next few years more LEA inner city and other urban schools will close or falter. Few of these at the moment will be predicting this unpleasant outcome. Too few, therefore, will act in time to avoid it unless they take the new task of marketing and promoting their school seriously in the way Baverstock and Small Heath have done.

The solution – general.   It is often only possible to sell a good product, but in today's world it is not sufficient to be good. A clear sense of continuing improvement and development must be generated and marketed.

The whole school must be involved in this process. It is not enough for senior management or even a staff and governors' committee to specialize in marketing. They need to lead and involve a willing, understanding staff and pupils who must all play their part. All must become conversant with the new culture and attitude, moreover, all must approve of it and enthusiastically implement it.

Promotion of the school is not a casual or optional extra but must be built into the whole school's development plan. It must be given a budget which is commensurate with the vital importance which promotion has for the survival and growth of the school.

It is important to signal that 'Under new management' or 'A new school for a new era and a new millennium' is the kind of image which is needed. The most modern customer-relations practices carry a code of conduct which is written and displayed in a visible location. The school should have one which is built into its mission statement. Quality control is now normally embodied in the school's development plan. But is it spelled out in simple terms for all visitors to see? It must become intimately related to the image of the school. The search for quality and for promotion must spur each other on.

The signposts of success

It was Marshall McLuhan who taught us that 'the medium is the message'. It is not what you actually say but the way you say it which conveys the content of your message to other people. Use the wrong medium and you can convey a message which is quite different from the one you wish to relay. We have already discussed how well-meaning teachers and administrators can send messages of failure and hostility to pupils rather than one of success. How can a school enshrine and disseminate the idea of the home, school and community working together to help each child to realize his or her full potential?

In a book which should be compulsory reading for all, *The Challenge of the Comprehensive School*, David Hargreaves (1982) outlines both the problem and some excellent solutions. So does Lord Elton (1989) in his compelling report, *Discipline in Schools*. His recommendations provide a vital way forward. With the help of some excellent guidelines from Coventry's community education advisers, the points of these authors can be summarized as follows:

The immediate signals which the school conveys must be positive:

- Is there a welcoming atmosphere? Is the visitor's first timid step inside the gate greeted with colour, warmth and hospitality?
- Are there welcoming signs in prominent places? Is the school's own crest and name proudly mounted above its main entry point?
- Is the school clearly and brightly signposted? Is it obvious where the offices of the secretary, head and home-link teacher are located? Do the children and staff greet the visitor with friendly smiles and with courtesy?
- Would a visitor immediately know where and who to turn to for help?
- What sort of reception does a telephone caller or a trades person receive?
- Do noticeboards and displays reflect a lively school with a range of quality academic as well as extracurricular activities? Are the corridors and walls filled with well-mounted work?
- Do they reflect the wider community in which the school is situated?
- Are the displays and notices up to date? Are the names of children clear? Are trophies, cups, school photographs and examination results displayed?
- Do furnishings, curtains and carpets indicate that it is a place for adults as well as children?

The quality of relationships can support or undermine initial perceptions.

1 *Relationships within the school*

- Does the school function as a whole, caring community?
- Do older pupils look after younger ones?
- Is there a positive relationship between:
  - the pupils themselves?
  - pupils and staff?
  - amongst the staff, including the non-teaching staff?
  - parents and the school?
  - the site users and the school?
- Is discipline and good conduct stressed as part of the school's moral code and the way the school itself functions as a whole community?

2 *Relationships between school and parents*

- How does the school form positive links with the parents before problems occur?
- Does the planning and style of open evenings enhance the relationships between parents and teachers?
- Are parents encouraged to contribute or to listen passively?
- How is account taken of parent's views?
- What opportunities exist for an ongoing dialogue with parents between open evenings?
- Are there mutually convenient arrangements for visiting – both home to school and school to home?
- What arrangements does the school have for written communications with parents? Are they clear and non-patronising?
- Is there a monthly or termly newsletter?
- Is there a parents room? How is it organized? Is this the only space for parents? Are they welcome in other parts of the school? Is there a room where parents can talk privately with members of staff?
- Is there a strategy which can deliver support to parents suffering from personal stress or worries over children?
- Is there knowledge and awareness of other agencies for referral? Where is this knowledge lodged and what form does it take?
- Are parents encouraged to take a direct part in helping teachers in the classroom and with extracurricular activities?
- Are parents involved in fund-raising activities, with school trips, and as local reference points and guides?
- Are older people, local employers and employees asked to visit the school to illustrate points of work, culture, history and geography?
- A nature or history trail or a bazaar can be used as an excuse for community involvement in the education of children.
- Are parents and residents encouraged to return to school to study in areas they failed to appreciate when they were of school age?

3 *Relationships between the school and other groups*

- Are the school facilities of plant, equipment and staff made available to parents and community groups:

- during the day?
- during the evening?
- during the weekend?
- during the school holidays?

- Are school children invited to take part in dual-use activities?
- Are there facilities for helping new groups to form and for supporting them?
- Are school and community uses kept separate or are the functions integrated?
- Do all staff share and support the policy of integration?
- Are the school secretary and caretaker able to answer questions and solve problems involving dual use?
- Is the head of school also head of centre?
- Is there a dual-use committee of users?
- Does the school curriculum and development plan incorporate the ethos of community education?

4 *Relationships between governors, parents, school and community*

- Are the names and photographs of governors prominently displayed? Is a public occasion made of governor elections?
- Are governors regular visitors to classrooms and the school's public occasions? Do they visit dual-use activities? Do different governors adopt different aspects of the school's life?
- Are reports presented to governors' meetings not just in writing or verbally, but with demonstrations and displays?
- Is the governors' annual report well printed and attractively designed as if it were a brochure to be used to market the school?
- Is the annual governors' meeting well presented? Is it just a formality with a few people in attendance? Or are many parents and community figures involved? Performances by classes, groups and clubs not only add a sense of fun, they can also graphically show all concerned the range of work being undertaken.
- Do the staff use governors' meetings and public occasions to help the 'nonexpert' parents and community representatives to become expert and confident in the process of governing the school?
- Above all, are the head and staff genuinely handing this government to the community and listening to its representatives' opinions and requests?
- Is the school truly a community school and the village hall of its community?

Discipline and moral maturity are not a problem in the urban self-governing school described above. As Lord Elton so eloquently elaborated in his report on discipline in schools, when discipline is fully integrated within a caring curriculum and in the context of the whole school, it begins to look after itself.

When Baverstock and Small Heath Schools became SG in 1989 they were taking a large step into the unknown. Few of the ways of managing schools described in this chapter had become a part of the common experience. Now, however, LM has helped most schools to begin to practise and benefit from the experience of partial autonomy. For them, the step to becoming fully self-governing should be short and relatively easy.

It is fitting to close this section with a quotation from Smith and Tomlinson (1989). Based on their study of 3,000 children in twenty comprehensive schools, they say: 'If schools were improved only within the current range of performance of urban comprehensive schools, this would be enough to transform the standards of secondary education' (p. 301). It is clearly very important to create the right conditions in which all schools can properly benefit their pupils. The next step in this task is to consider the curriculum of the good independent state school.

REFERENCES

Coventry LEA *Community Education Briefings*. Internal publication.
Elton, Lord (1989) *Discipline in Schools*. London: HMSO.
Hargreaves, D. (1982) *The Challenge of the Comprehensive School*. London: Routledge & Kegan Paul.
Hargreaves, D. and Hopkins, D. (1991) *The Empowered School*. London: Cassell.
Perks, Roger. Private conversations and papers.
The Phoenix Journal (1993). Birmingham: The Phoenix Centre.
Ree, H. (1985) *Educator Extraordinary*. London: Peter Owen.
Smith, D. and Tomlinson, S. (1989) *The School Effect*. London: Policy Studies Institute.

Chapter 8

A New Curriculum

In the past, many educational administrators have assumed that the unlucky 80 per cent were not capable of benefiting from and acquiring the academic virtues of the good school. They concluded that because such pupils were clearly not academic, they should be offered only 'practical' subjects like woodwork, metalwork and, more recently, craft, design and technology which would enable them to bid for today's technological equivalent of yesterday's manual job. Worse, it became possible to suggest that two quite different schools with different educational content should be offered: good and academic, and poor and practical. The thinking is well intentioned but likely only to short-change the 80 per cent. It makes three basic mistakes.

It assumes that most people do not have the 'cognitive intelligence' required to perform on a par with the best. It assumes that the education of the elite does not need further revision and the incorporation of the practical touch. It assumes that the curriculum of the community school in the inner and outer city areas cannot be made academically exciting for pupils as well as practical.

The self-governing community school must redress this balance. It is now necessary to look at the new kind of curriculum which the new good school should offer if it is to enable the 80 per cent to challenge and reach the heights of the 20 per cent and to provide the nation with the highly intelligent and motivated workforce which it needs to survive and compete in the modern world, and to provide the community with the self-possessed, caring individuals it needs if it is to become spirited.

Those who see community education as a 'bolt-on' extra to the 'real' 9 a.m. to 3.30 p.m. task of education which schools can take or leave, also tend to see the community education curriculum in similar terms. To them, community education is to be measured in terms of adult evening classes and dual-use activities. From such a standpoint it is difficult to find a serious or central place in the school's curriculum for community education. Indeed, the only location which can be found is in peripheral, optional community studies' visits to old people and a local survey of, say, shopping facilities. In so far as community education is admitted into the curriculum, it is done so from the standpoint that it is a 'subject' to be studied, like others, with a 'place' allotted to it on the timetable. As such, it is not surprising to find that it is thought to be

more suitable for entertaining those 'not up to' the study of real and serious academic subjects.

This view has quite rightly led some to question the validity of existing definitions of community education. This is sad, for the new kind of community school also calls for a much more robust and effective view of community education in relation to the curriculum. It is seen not as an optional extra subject but at the very core of the curriculum. It is the integrating factor in the national curriculum which all schools must teach.

The community-centred approach to education sees the community which surrounds school as a multifaceted resource, a living, working textbook through which the whole of the curriculum can be brought to life and made meaningful and exciting to teachers as well as pupils and parents. Community-oriented education is not a subject which requires a timetabled place on the curriculum. It is the catalyst which makes the whole timetable attractive and integrates an otherwise segregated, disjointed curriculum.

What is education if not the means by which the individual reflects on his or her existing (community-derived) experience and talents, works on them, dissects them and puts them together again in fresh ways in order to make sense of the world? It is the means by which to gain appreciation of, and mastery over life. Education in this sense is a means to greater self and communal awareness in order to enable the individual to live a purposeful adult, family, working and recreational life. It is a project whose aim is to make life more enriching and fulfilling, and as such, the different 'subject' divisions of a curriculum like maths, English and science are merely separate pieces of a jigsaw puzzle which only make sense when put together into the whole picture of life. The separate subjects will only command interest and motivate genuine study when the student can see them not as a separate fragment but as part of the total picture which would be incomplete without that fragment. Perhaps, at a later, more advanced stage, 'pure' study in one or other special area may capture the interest of the mature student. But in the early years and through much of primary and secondary schooling, education can either be the mind-numbing uncomprehending learning of facts and figures or it can become a joyful act of work which deepens the students' understanding of self, their situation and the surrounding world. In this context, the relationship between student and teacher comes to resemble that between apprentice and expert craftsperson.

The national Schools Curriculum Awards are becoming coveted prizes. John Tomlinson, President of the Society of Education Officers, outlined the objects of the awards and in doing so, he began to spell out just how the curriculum can be enriched for pupils and their teachers by the community which surrounds the school. Tomlinson wrote (1983):

> The object of the award is to identify and celebrate schools which have established a broad and balanced curriculum enriched from the local community and environment. Such schools will have resisted the temptation to narrow their activities and will have strengthened their capacity to introduce children to their social and cultural heritage by acting with the community and drawing upon its resources. The central question will be: is this school, in its particular situation, passively accepting limitations (real or imagined), or is it imaginatively using the resources to hand?
>
> There is a great deal of experience to show how schools may use their environment as an instrument of education – in visual education, the arts, social and biological studies, industrial and commercial studies, history, geography, technological studies, careers education and in bringing adults into the schools as well as by taking pupils outside the school

building. There is a vast difference between the school that ignores its environment and the one which draws strength from it.

We are not thinking of a particular project but a practical philosophy. We are seeking schools which have learned how to live out their ideas. Such schools will not only have given their pupils a firm grasp of the basic skills, but will also be helping them to use and develop those skills in the context of experience. We would also hope to find that such schools enjoyed their work and were appreciated by their community.

Immediate experience raises questions about events and circumstances that occurred in the past, or happen elsewhere, or are products of an artist's or an author's mind and hand. But it is direct experience that provides the scale against which accounts from a distance or the interpretations of others may be set. Study and activity based on the locality, then, does not diminish the importance of literacy and numeracy, or of learning about historical and geographical events and conditions, or of literature and other works of imagination: quite the contrary. Well-guided involvement with local happenings, circumstances and conditions enhance and extend skills and provide keys for understanding which cannot be directly experienced.

Many schools have experience in working with their local communities. Such co-operation is not the product of any particular school or community; it does not have to be the creation of a rich or poor environment, urban or rural; nor is it the possession of any race, religion or age group. It is part of the climate or ethos of the school and the willingness of the community to co-operate.

The awards scheme seeks to identify schools involved in a community's structure and work. This could be expected to include:

- The natural and built environment, its use in visual and general education. The problem of awakening a community's concern for the appearance of its environment and ways in which it can be improved and enriched.
- The local economy, how wealth is created and distributed within the local community. Changing patterns of employment, opportunities for new businesses, unemployment and the implications of all this for the school.
- The social structure, including care and advice available to different groups – religious groups, political parties, trade unions, clubs, etc. The organized action of the different social institutions. Centres of influence within the community.
- The culture, the history and traditions, art, music, dance and drama, and uses of leisure.

The submission should be a practical expression of the ethos of the school as a whole – the particular enthusiasm of one teacher and one group of pupils will not be enough. It should, where appropriate, use the skills and knowledge of people in the local community as well as those of the pupils and include activity on the part of pupils working with and for members of the community.

It should show evidence of doing, making and working together. It should be clear how this involvement has been used by pupils and teachers to enrich the curriculum and reinforce the development of basic skills. From the community angle, it should be possible to discern improvements for the community and for the general relationships with and understanding of young people.

Shouldn't every school prepare its curriculum with the same careful and structured thought? Shouldn't every school build the community education approach into its school development plan and review progress on a rigorous and regular basis? Shouldn't that plan not just include the approach to the timetabled curriculum outlined above, but also the whole school approach outlined in the earlier description of the school itself and the messages it sends to pupils, parents and community?

John Watts, ex-head of Countesthorp School, is writing a book about memorable teaching moments. He makes the point that just about everyone can recall an occasion in their life of which they can say: 'At that moment I learned something really valuable from that person. It has helped me in later life. I shall never forget either the moment or the teacher.'

How many of these moments, John Watts asks, take place in a formal lesson? Not as many, he suggests, as those which take place on the playing field, in the home, on an outing, whilst doing a holiday job. How many of these moments of inspired teaching and learning involve a qualified teacher? Again, John Watts suggests, not as many as those which involve a member of the family, a sports coach, a chance meeting or a work setting. Could the precious moment have been an act of self-discovery or one gained whilst playing with a group of young friends?

The intriguing questions which John Watts goes on to pose are: 'How do you analyse these moments? . . . What do they have in common? . . . From the answers to these questions is it possible to begin to pose a way of learning which can be of great value to teachers and schools?'

The book is not yet complete, so we will have to wait for an answer, but most of us know that it is not just the educational 'failure' for whom these moments do not occur in school but in 'real' life. For almost all of us they did not occur in the classroom. If they did occur in a school setting it is most likely to have happened in an extracurricular context, and the 'significant other' might as easily have been a fellow pupil as a teacher. But, it remains likely that a very high percentage of us would choose to recount an experience which had nothing at all to do with school. Put it another way, when John Watts produces his set of teaching methods derived from a host of memorable occasions, will it be easy to incorporate them into the existing school curriculum and to replicate them in the classroom setting?

Something has to give. It is not just the 'failure' for whom school as it exists has proved a colossal and expensive waste of time. It could be that the large majority, even the 'academic' high fliers, are missing out on some very important lessons indeed. What are these lessons? How can they be taught? There are two different but inter-related ways of answering these questions. One way can be called 'project performance and problem solving'. The other can be termed 'intelligence, a case of mistaken identity'.

Project performance and problem solving

Rather than attempting to teach exclusively by means of artificially discrete subject areas, it is often sensible to teach by taking problems which occur in the real world and asking pupils to solve them or by setting them projects to accomplish. Five examples follow.

Example I

In *The Challenge of the Comprehensive School*, David Hargreaves (1982) chooses drama with which to make this point. He writes that:

In the performance of a play there is a highly elaborate distribution and specialization of labour: there are actors, with large and small parts; a stage staff of those who build and paint scenery, lighting technicians, dress designers and so on; a house staff who deal with programmes, tickets and refreshments. It is like a society in miniature, with its differentiation of function, and some participants having more central roles than others. But for a play to be successful, each contributor must give of his best and be correctly integrated with all the other elements. [If the person with the smallest contribution to make] fluffs his lines or is neglectful of his contribution, the enterprise as a whole is in danger of being ruined. Anyone who has been involved with a school play production knows what a tremendous and exciting corporate spirit is generated, particularly just before and during the public performance. It is an exemplar of differentiated team work

(p. 105)

which is like that of a real-world agency or business. It makes the relationship of pupil and teacher more like the real-world one of apprentice and expert craftsperson.

Individual performers may be outstanding and get credit for it. But the success of a few does not, as happens in classrooms, automatically generate a sense of failure in the rest. Those with more lowly contributions know perfectly well that they could not be the 'star' of the show, but they know that they have been making a contribution which is essential to the whole enterprise and which is thus known to be valued. A play thus gives the participants dignity ... Each makes a contribution, the competent execution of which brings a sense of being valued. Solidarity and dignity are conferred simultaneously.

(p. 152)

'Character' and 'quality' are taught, so too is the excitement of learning how to meet real problems, possibilities, deadlines which result in the experience and delight of achievement.

Example II

Every teacher can see the virtue in a school pond or greenhouse or a visit to a local river bank. An obvious wealth of botanical and zoological information abounds there which can be brought back into the classroom to trigger further study. It does not so easily occur to them that an even greater wealth of material can be found in the local council housing estate. Central government recognizes that estates built in the 1940s and 1950s need to be refurbished. The City of Birmingham's Housing Department has two hundred and fifty million pounds with which to tackle several of its decaying estates. The Cock Hill estate which surrounds Colmers Farm Nursery, Infant, Junior and Secondary schools is one of these and between ten and twenty million pounds is to be spent on this estate over the next few years. But how is the spending to be allocated? How is the refurbishment to be planned? How can the residents take part in the planning and execution of the plan so that their 'new' estate is to their liking? There are three different aspects to this project.

1 *The schools could help with the planning process which results in a plan for the estate by:*

- Acting as gatherers of information and opinion about the estate.
- Asking residents what is right with the estate which needs strengthening.

- Asking residents what is wrong with the estate which needs amending or rebuilding.
- Addressing the problems of litter, graffiti and uncared for open spaces.
- Wondering what factors can help build community spirit, a sense of security, self help and neighbourliness.
- Building a scale model of the estate as it is, then inviting pupils and parents to move the items about to help them get a real feel of the planning process.
- The school acting as the base for a community architect while the architect draws up the estate plans with the help of the above suggestions.

2 *Once the plan is in place, the school could track, study and participate in the rebuilding work:*

- A fair part of the building process and the trades required could be studied – carpentry, plumbing, roofing, etc.
- The architecture, the quantity surveying and quality control could be included in these studies.
- It would equally be important to consider the effects of the dislocation to the life of families caused by the rebuilding and the means of easing them.
- There is much core curriculum English, maths and science in this as well as business studies and administration.
- In addition to the pure study which comes from this project, the school could also build or help to build a parent/community room or resource centre in its grounds. Could the school be refurbished as part of the estate plan?
- Just how much hands-on work experience is possible in such a project is determined more by the will and imagination of the school than by any other obstacle.

3 *How is the estate to be maintained?*

- Can the local school make room for the otherwise centrally based housing officer?
- Could the schools generally be available to officers from different city departments to hold advice sessions and become 'neighbourhood offices'?
- Could a school's environmental studies course be related to estate management and maintenance so that a sense of belonging is deepened? Could some of that main-tenance be undertaken by the school?
- Could the school win a maintenance contract for part of the estate and be paid for studying whilst working?
- Could the school help the housing department's staff to produce a tenants' news-paper and jointly assist with the drawing up of community profiles and agendas to urge upon their own and other departments? The estate will need to develop and grow rather than remain static. Good maintenance is a part of growth and development.

There is more education than meets the eye in housing estates. A school project which entails the whole school taking part in the twenty million pounds refurbishment of the estate, in which its pupils live, is a potential delight for pupils, teachers and community alike. Real work experience and education are combined. Just as St. Paul's brings Language Alive!, surely there can be no better way than this to bring maths, science, technology, architecture, administration, social studies and commerce to life.

Example III

Nearly every school is close to a dreadful, derelict patch of land which no one looks after and which resembles a local tip. Pupils have to pass it every day. It undermines their own esteem of their home and the public image of their community. It is one reason why their teacher probably lives elsewhere and will move to a better school as soon as possible.

Surely there is nothing in this rubbish tip which is worth studying? Surely if someone should do anything about the site it is someone other than the school, teacher or pupil? Wrong, actually, as the whole world and much of the experience of the pupil is captured in that site.

First, let us look at it face on, rather than hurry past. It is awful isn't it? How did it get that way? Why is it tolerated? Why do others make it worse?

Second, what was the site originally? Did houses once stand there? Before the houses were built, was it a field? Do the roads still conform to field boundaries? Who farmed there? Who bought the farms to build the houses and who lived in those houses? Why were the houses knocked down? What plans now exist in city centre offices for some future development?

Third, where has the rubbish come from? Why is it that some modern manufacturing processes make waste disposal difficult? What are the modern systems of waste disposal? Can newer, better ways be devised? How did people dispose of waste in the past? Haven't archaeologists found that waste helpful? Could we become modern archaeologists?

Fourth, can rubbish be used to create art? What art can be created from the debris of a forest and the debris of a community? Might some of our modern processes of manufacture have to change if our environment is to be well cared for? What kinds of art forms might we decorate our community with? How can we construct a statue? Shall we make one?

Fifth, if we could clear the site what would we do with it? Would we turn it into a mini-park or build new houses on it? Who could we ask to help us clear it and what materials would we need to landscape it into a park? Will they visit and talk to us? How much money would we need and how could we raise it?

The impossible and the unthinkable suddenly become both thinkable and possible. In place of a tip there is an attractive little park, and a sense of achievement and pride. The different academic disciplines which need to be brought to bear on the study range from maths and English through history, geography and science to a study of manufacturing processes and environmental issues in which either just one or two classes or a whole school could be involved.

Finally, imagine the drama and publicity which could be made out of the official opening with residents, shopkeepers, parents and dignitaries to unveil the statue, with all those who helped put the mini-park on the map in attendance. There is scope for music and stalls, the local radio, a write-up in the local press and a plea to all concerned to make even greater efforts to improve the image of the area. And it is all education mixed up with real life, but, at the end of the day it is as academic as you can get and for *all* of the pupils.

Example IV

It has always been possible to learn many lessons from the great outdoors. 'Outward Bound' courses are not the exclusive province of those public schools to which royalty sends its male children. Such courses have come to be of interest to all kinds of schools. They are also increasingly favoured by managers of companies who need to develop in their colleagues the qualities of interdependence, team work, initiative and character, which are not always taught in school. Philip Schofield wrote that these 'away' courses help people to understand their 'abilities, limitations and motivations'. They 'develop confidence in coping with new situations. They aim to improve communication, leadership' and to develop skills in 'analysing problems, assessing options, making decisions and taking calculated risks'.

Philip Schofield describes a typical course which was laid on for a new management team from British Aerospace in the Lake District by J. B. Norman and Associates:

> This was a mountain rescue in which a participant was lowered on a stretcher down a 60 ft vertical cliff interrupted midway by a ledge. The stretcher was lowered by two ropes, each handled by someone perched on the cliff ledge. The stretcher was accompanied by a 'barrow boy' lowered on a third rope to control the stretcher's descent and steer it past each obstacle on the way. Because the rope handlers at the top lost sight and sound of the stretcher and the barrow boy once past the ledge, one person was lowered and anchored to the ledge to relay communications.
>
> Much became obvious through this experience: the need to preplan each step, to prepare equipment and to know one's individual responsibilities before starting to lower the 'casualty' over the cliff. The need for lucid communications was apparent as the barrow boy called instructions to each rope handler, and for part of the time through the relay on the ledge. And because the task carried real risks all were aware of the need to follow safety procedures and for fail-safe systems.
>
> The rescue was a complete management exercise – from briefing, planning resource and task allocation, through implementation, coping with problems as they arose, to an outcome – all in 90 minutes. A workplace project usually takes weeks and is interrupted by unrelated tasks and problems; the lessons are less clear-cut.

Trudi Wakeman, a trainer who organizes such courses in Cumbria, suggests that people 'gain an awareness of their own leadership style, develop the ability to offer constructive feedback to others, learn to look at achievements in personal terms not as competition against others.' This means of learning through 'practical experience' is reminiscent of what John Watts had in mind when considering memorable learning moments which all too often occur outside the formal educational process. If that process can be broadened to take into account 'Outward Bound' and a whole series of 'voluntary service' type experiences then the distinction between formal education and real life could be effectively breached.

Example V

Man does not live by bread alone. On those occasions when people have tried to manage for any length of time without a moral centre to their lives difficulties have been encountered. In this sense it is idle philosophy to imagine that it is possible to

choose whether to be moral or amoral. For man is, by definition, a social, spiritual being.

Each child cannot develop into a well-balanced adult without being provided, by parents, teachers and community, with a clear framework of rules, a code of conduct, by which to relate to others, as well as a set of values which integrate, inform and make internally consistent this set of rules. These values provide the central and over-arching meaning to life. Neither school nor community can be neutral about or ignore these rules and values. Indeed, as each school functions as a small social as well as an educational community it needs to practise, live by and reflect its own clear rules and values, which must be consistent with and celebrate those of the wider community within which the school is located.

In this sense, the whole of school life, whether in class or out of it, including its method of discipline, is a key participatory project in the preparation of the child for adult life in the community. In addition to teaching a variety of discrete subject areas and projects, school must assist the child with the development of character and a sense of morality. While religious instruction might occupy a few periods a week, every aspect of the organization and practical experience of the school's life must concern character development and the acquisition of values through which the quality of life can be judged and influenced.

Too often today the state school has ignored the spiritual side of life to the detriment of both the atmosphere and sense of purpose of the school and the level of maturity of its pupils. Discipline, regard for others and for self can be too lax. Study and educational standards can suffer as a consequence. A good school is a moral school. In this sense the final illustration of project work, which it is important to detail, is the all-encompassing one of daily conduct, relationships and morality.

Intelligence – a case of mistaken identity

'Learning to learn' is too rarely addressed. Like speech it is generally assumed that children will simply 'pick it up'. Or, more often, the ability to learn is equated with intelligence which cannot be learned but is inherited. Either way, it is assumed that pupils come to school with the ability to learn already acquired. It need not be taught. Pupils who then don't learn the 'facts' or 'lessons' which are taught to them are thought by their teachers to be 'unintelligent' and in future are addressed and taught accordingly. Professor Feuerstein, an Israeli educational psychologist and teacher has clearly shown this to be a misconception.

He has shown that 'intelligence' or the ability to learn is not just innate, but is also learned. Many people do indeed acquire it naturally in their early years, but others, whose early years may have been deficient, need to be explicitly taught how to learn, how to arrange and order facts to make sense of the world. Feuerstein (quoted in Sharron, 1988) has shown how both 'backward' and 'able' children can enhance their measured IQ considerably as a result of being taught how to learn.

The problems which the production of a play presents are not unlike those which Feuerstein uses to help children learn to learn and find joy in the learning process. This new-found ability and the pleasure it gives can then be equally applied to any subject area. The teacher who previously 'found Jack to be a dull boy' when given

only formal subject work to do can be very pleasantly surprised to find that the school/community play gave him the educational kiss of life.

David Hargreaves happened to choose a drama project to illustrate his point. He could just as easily have chosen other topics, for example, the school orchestra, a carnival, a school expedition or field-study trip, or a craft, design and technology exercise such as building a motorized go-cart or a pond for the nursery. Each project is a task and end in itself which is real and challenging, but each demands the use of arithmetical, written and verbal linguistic skills, and the use of a host of subject areas. Yet in the context of a project, as in real life, these are the means to a greater, more exciting end. In ordinary school life they too often appear as the end itself and seem irrelevant to the world outside the classroom.

We are beginning to think of intelligence in a way which differs from the academic concept of it. First, intelligence can be acquired and improved upon. It can be taught. Had St Paul's pupils all stayed at their state school they would have left with no examination results. Like Feuerstein's pupils they showed that in a different setting they could perform rather better than had previously been expected.

Second, it manifests itself in different qualities and walks of life. The star performer in the drama may be a 'dunce' at arithmetic. The good footballer turns movement into an art form, but may not be too good with words. The professor may be adept at the various uses of literacy but not very good at football. Who earns the money? Who pulls in the crowds? Who, therefore, in his or her wake creates a thousand jobs?

The academic concept of intelligence places the professor at the top of the pyramid. The standpoint we are advocating suggests that both the professor and the good footballer manifest intelligence in different ways. Society finds both forms to be of use. Its broader judgement is rather more telling than that of the narrow, self-interested academic one which has traditionally denied and confused this common-sense, everyday definition of 'brightness'.

The academic view of intelligence has done a great deal of mischief, both to the pupil and to society, for it has relegated other forms of intelligence to an extra-curricular role or ignored them all together. Had it not done so, a great many 'failures' would have found pride and confidence in their non-academic skills well before they discovered it by chance in their later life as John Watts points out. Society would benefit by receiving from schools a great many more confident and recognized adults who did not need to await a chance encounter with one of John Watts' non-teacher teachers. How can intelligences other than the academic or 'cognitive intellectual' be distinguished and catered for?

David Hargreaves recognizes four additional types of intelligence which he feels are all equally relevant and important for life in the real world, but which are played down in the school curriculum. They are the:

- Aesthetic/artistic
- Affective/emotional
- Physical/manual
- Personal/social

Of course, these qualities cannot be completely removed from the life of a school. But Hargreaves (1982) points out that:

those school subjects in which they have a particularly strong ... significance, such as art, craft, music, woodwork, drama and physical education ... tend to appear on the timetable in the lowly status of one-period-a-week subjects and, as pupils become older, to become optional subjects ... The hidden curriculum message is clear: the only knowledge and skills which really count in school ... are primarily intellectual-cognitive in content (p. 52),

in which only a few can be expected to excel and find enjoyment.

A similar point is made by Charles Handy (1989). He says that:

Society today sieves people in their late teens. The clever ones (the 20 per cent) go on to further studies and qualifications, the rest (the 80 per cent) are left to fend for themselves. We only use one sieve, that of intellectual achievement as measured by examination.

Charles Handy points out that in order to grow, modern communities need more skills and talents than raw intellect alone and that most people have at least one skill or talent other than academic intelligence, and that most, therefore, have a saleable skill or ability which school fails to acknowledge and nurture.

Howard Gardner of the Harvard School of Education recognizes more of these qualities than Hargreaves. He classifies seven different types of talents, each of which can be measured and taught from an early age providing that the curriculum and organization of schools are geared to their development and enrichment. His seven talents, as summarized by Handy, include:

- *Analytic intelligence*: the sort measured in IQ tests and examinations which overwhelmingly dominates education at every level.
- *Pattern intelligence*: the ability to see patterns in things and to create patterns. Mathematicians, artists, computer programmers often have this intelligence to a high degree.
- *Musical intelligence*: possessed by both people who play instruments and large swathes of the population who listen attentively. Analytically clever they may not be, musically intelligent they undoubtedly are.
- *Physical intelligence*: possessed by swimmers, footballers and sporting people of all kinds but no guarantee of any other kind of intelligence.
- *Practical intelligence*: the ability to take a TV set or motor car engine apart and put it together again so that it works. Its possessor can't necessarily spell the names of the moving parts or write eloquently about them.
- *Intrapersonal intelligence*: shown by the poet and the counsellor who may be quiet and self-effacing but are in tune with the feelings and needs of others.
- *Interpersonal intelligence*: the ability to get on with others and get things done through them. It is shown by managers and organizers.

All these qualities and abilities have a vital place in life, both in work and in the home and community. As Handy says, 'If we look around in middle age at the people who are happy and successful we see it is because they have found what they are good at and are doing it.' They or their non-teacher teacher somehow managed to discover what school entirely missed. Too often this discovery was made by the individual alone, or with the help of a chance learning experience of the kind which John Watts describes rather than with the help of school. But it should be possible to make

school life more attractive, more adept at recognizing and building upon the strength of its pupils, so that education is no longer haphazard but the deliberate and joyful product of that very expensive period of each pupil's life from five years of age to sixteen plus.

If we are to help all pupils to reach their full potential, and not just the existing 20 per cent, then a refinement must be made to Hargreaves', Handy's and Gardner's views of the different kinds of aptitude and intelligence. For they are in danger of continuing the myth that only a very few people are capable of the cognitive-intellectual or analytical intelligence and that it is of the same status as all the other manifestations of intelligence or ways of seeing and making a living in life. Surely cognitive intelligence – the ability to learn – holds an unrecognized but pivotal role in bringing all other forms of learning to fruition, thus enabling each pupil to gain control over his or her particular subject or area of interest?

The successful musician, footballer and manager will all need to acquire, rehearse, refine and develop a fluency over their cognitive intelligence if they are to reflect effectively on what they are doing, then extend and improve upon it. It would be a great mistake if at the very moment of breaking the university-dominated mystique and dominance over intelligence it was to be handed back unrefined and unreformed. On the contrary, all can benefit from the best of the academic university tradition. We merely need to reform the ways of introducing the previously excluded 80 per cent of the population to its benefits and relevance to all aspects of life.

Individual subjects

It is helpful to highlight the potentially dynamic interrelationship between individual subject work and project, performance-oriented work. The use, need and value of a subject can be made meaningful to the pupil through project work because it can be revealed as a vital, functioning ingredient of that project.

It then becomes possible to extract the subject artificially from the living whole as an object worthy of further, more detailed study. For a more advanced grasp of the subject will enable more complex projects to be tackled and appreciated more fully in the future. By subject we now, of course, mean not just maths and English, but music, organization, leadership and all those areas of intelligence outlined above.

Getting the balance right between the study of individual subjects and project work is important. To take a subject away from its context and meaning in the real world for too long can swiftly become counterproductive. Similarly, to concentrate only on project work can run the risk that the development of a deeper understanding is inhibited. It too will eventually become counterproductive.

In order to consider how best to get the balance right it is helpful, for a moment, to think of physical education leading to team work and vice versa. Various exercises in the gym are important. They can be made enjoyable in addition to hard work by adding music and movement to them as well as team games designed to exercise arm or leg or back muscles. It is then possible to study the skeleton and the way muscles work. But the object of these exercises is, say, the performance of a team in competition with other teams in the field.

When it first performs the team is not as well co-ordinated or as effective as it might be. It is necessary to go back to the drawing board, practise short sprints, ball control, group collaborative work, etc. which involve concentration, lateral thinking and discipline. After a while, the team is ready for a second performance. Again, slips and mistakes which are made during the game are clearly seen as needing the remedy of further repetition and hard training work.

This quick analogy of the relationship between specific study and training on the one hand, and the performance of the actual game on the other, is applicable to every subject area and every kind of project. Direct parallels can be drawn with the school drama which we outlined. The same can be said of the environmental work on estate and derelict sites which we looked at. Each study could be initiated by setting the project as the first goal, from which the individual subject studies took wing or they could be arrived at from the need to apply the individual study of maths or English, carpentry or management in the real life, working setting of the project.

Yet, traditionally it is the artificially isolated cognitive-intellectual subjects which have occupied pride of place on the timetable. The real life, enjoyable project which potentially gives real meaning to all subjects has been too often relegated to the extracurricular optional extra. Once community education is seen as the defining feature of the school, and the integrating factor in the curriculum, it is possible to realign that balance, make school real to its pupils and recognize that cognitive intelligence is not the special possession of a privileged 20 per cent or even of academic subjects alone but is accessible to all pupils and all disciplines. Redressing the balance and recognizing the universal application of the cognitive-intellectual dimension establishes two important possibilities.

The first possibility concerns the school's relationship with the community which we began to address whilst discussing the nature of the community school. Now that the content and style of the curriculum has been added to the equation we can see that the community school can function as a kind of complex working apprenticeship for adult life. It can, indeed it must, perform a whole series of useful projects/tasks from which the community benefits – plays, concerts, environmental improvement, designing and helping rebuild estates – the list is endless. Of course the school cannot perform these feats alone. Adult experts from the community need to be brought in to give advice. Other agencies, real businesses and city departments need to be involved, but the community school functions as the focal point, the hub of the wheel for all these different people and groups. It becomes the dynamo which drives and brings light and enlightenment to communal life. Indeed, it sets the scene and makes the vital contribution to these communal celebrations of spirit and identity at such times as midsummer, Christmas, bonfire night and other suitable occasions. The school is the village hall on the village green. The school is the contemporary Shakespearian Globe Theatre of its community.

The second possibility concerns pure intellect of whatever kind and the study of a subject which is not just a part of a wider project and real life, but becomes a pure pursuit in its own right. Once brought to life, not by chance but by design, it is possible to imagine that more pupils will see the point and feel the excitement in taking, say, the electricity or information technology in stage lighting, the physics in movement, the English in communication, the maths in business, the composition in a concert and the morality in the organization of school and community life

as far as they will go. The list is as endless as there are distinct, or groups of, subjects.

Far from reducing the value of the study of individual subjects, the community school's curriculum enhances them and must provide vital facilities for them including a bold place on the timetable for advanced and sixth-form study. The key distinction between the more traditional school and the community school is the equal value which is afforded by the latter to a range of 'subjects' and projects which reflect the full range of intelligences, all of which are underpinned by a new-found ability to experience the excitement of learning.

Equal respect must be paid to pattern, musical, physical, practical, intrapersonal and interpersonal intelligences and to the fact that analytical intelligence is equally relevant to all areas of understanding but no one school alone is likely to be able to cater fully for all of these. A school may well lean in one direction or another or, perhaps, in two or three directions rather than all of them.

It is important for parents not to be offered the meaningless choice between a good and a bad school, for who would not choose the good school if they could? Rather, parents would respond well to having to choose between schools which are renowned centres of excellence in physical pursuits or musical ones or analytical ones. Each school will wish to stress the particular cluster of subjects in which it specializes. These will not, of course, lead to that school's exclusion of the other subjects. Rather they will be taught in the wake of, and to make sense of, the specialist ones. Such specialism will make it more likely that the next poet or business genius or contented adult arises not by accident but as a result of the deliberate support given to particular talents.

Striking the right balance between project and subject-oriented work in an integrated community education curriculum will not be achieved overnight. The interrelationship between school and community will deepen and the school will become the hub around which much of the life and work of the community turns. Exciting, but difficult. 'How can we achieve it when we have so many other considerations such as going SG and implementing the national curriculum?' will be the common plea and question of teachers. There are four answers to this point, each of them equally telling.

1 Self-government can only properly be implemented by turning the school into the community school. They are not separate exercises. They are one and the same task.

2 The same point applies to the national curriculum. Taught in the traditional way it could seem dull, hard work and fall on the unreceptive ears of pupils, especially the less obviously academic ones. Using the community as a living textbook through which to teach the curriculum adds spice and enthusiasm. The implementation of the national curriculum is most easily and rewardingly achieved by using the community as the integrating factor which gives meaning to subjects and illustrates their interconnection which helps the community to develop.

3 The doubter needs to recall that we are advocating that the existing centralized local education authority (LEA) bureaucracy should be delegated out to individual schools. Chapter 10 discusses how a part of that delegation can be used to help staff to teach in the way outlined above and to provide them with the ideas, packs, introductions and resources which could make teaching both a joy and a vital community asset.

4   Each school would benefit from the presence of an experienced community education specialist to help guide it through any transition phases. The role of this
specialist will be explored in the next chapter, for it will be crucially important
in helping existing schools to move from the ethos and style of the uniformity of
the off-the-peg 'state school' to that of the self-governing 'community school' as
a centre of excellence.

REFERENCES

Hardy, C. (1989) *The Age of Unreason*. London: Hutchinson.
Hargreaves, D. (1982) *The Challenge of the Comprehensive School*. London: Routledge &
    Kegan Paul.
Sharron, H. (1988) *Changing Children's Minds*. London: Souvenir.
Tomlinson, J. (1983) *The Schools Curriculum Awards*.

This chapter also uses material from private conversations with John Watts and Peter Simpson.

Chapter 9

A New Teacher

If the new school is to become fully independent it not only needs a community education curriculum, it also needs a new teacher. However, helping a new teacher to emerge from the dependency culture is neither easy nor straightforward. In the first four years following the 1988 education legislation no school or set of teachers have been invited to become independent by its LEA. Most of the schools which have individually chosen autonomy did so because their parents and governors voted to opt out of LEA control. With the exception of heads and senior staff, however, most teachers were at first 'instinctively' against the move and anxious because it did not have their existing (LEA) employer's blessing. The teachers' unions are, of course, vehemently against self-government because of the blow this strikes at their institutional relationship with the LEAs. So it is understandable that teachers at first recoil from autonomy and are uncertain about how to put it into practice. How can they be helped to overcome these reservations?

At first glance it might make sense to turn for assistance to those teachers who are already designated 'community education specialists'. Perhaps they can reassure their colleagues not only that independence offers security but that it can provide a variety of advantages for them, their pupils and their school.

However, just as in the past community education has often been marginalized into bolt-on, dual-use activities or worthy visits to old people, so also have previous attempts to create the community education teacher been diverted from the mainstream educational activities of schools into peripheral pursuits. Some primary schools have pre-school workers (PSWs) whose task is to specialize in helping the parents of pre-school children become familiar and at ease with the expectations of schools. Their task is also designed to help teachers become more aware of the educational potential of the family and gain confidence in working with parents. Some primary and secondary schools also have home–school liaison teachers (HSLTs). Their tasks are similar to those of PSWs. The basic aim of HSLTs and PSWs is to find and develop the links between home and school but some heads have used these potentially valuable specialists as extra pairs of hands to help out with ordinary teaching duties. Other heads have become complacent in the knowledge that their solitary 'specialist' is 'doing' the school's home–school link

duties. So 'ordinary' teachers in the school, who might otherwise have visited their pupils' homes, attended community functions or helped to develop the community education curriculum, are encouraged to refer their own community education duties to the 'specialist'. It is, therefore, possible for a school which has a specialist community education teacher to have a less effective community education programme than one which does not.

Such developments are often compounded because community education can too easily become identified solely with 'visiting home' when the child is absent from school or for some other negative reason such as bad conduct. So, HSLTs can be seen as troubleshooters as well as 'extra pairs of hands'. It is little wonder that underutilized, ill-managed HSLTs have too frequently come to see themselves as occupying dead-end jobs which have neither status nor prospects. The best and most committed teachers have consequently avoided these posts and the potential of community education has remained hidden to them and their school.

Thus, many existing community education staff do not have either the experience, interest or status to help them to persuade their colleagues to enter wholeheartedly into the spirit of the new school. This is disappointing because each headteacher does need at least one close and senior ally to help them to gain the confidence of all staff if their school is to move smoothly towards the new culture of self-government. In the absence of a community education specialist the head will need the active support of a deputy or an enthusiastic member of the senior management team. Their post might be retitled independent community education specialist (ICES). The role of the ICES can be outlined as follows:

General aims of the ICES

- To enable the whole school to become an independent community school in association with its neighbours and to raise standards.
- To help all teachers develop a community education philosophy, commitment, curriculum and practice which pervades all aspects of the school's life, welcomes home and community into the school and takes the school out into the community.
- To develop mutual understanding and support between school, family and community to the educational benefit of the pupils, teachers, parents and the wider community.

Duties and responsibilites with teachers in classrooms

- Through a direct teaching commitment and position within the senior management team to help colleagues to develop and practise a community education-oriented way of teaching the national curriculum.
- To work with colleagues on common, whole-school and inter-school projects.
- To enhance colleagues' awareness of the diverse needs, attitudes and values of pupils and the means by which parents and community figures can assist with the teaching process and play a more direct and confident role in the education of their own and other children.

- To play a direct role in helping the management of the school to enhance the educational standards within the school.
- In the case of primary schools to help some staff pay particular attention to the needs of the pre-school child and ease the transition of the child from primary to secondary school.
- In the case of secondary schools to help some staff assist with the transition of the child from primary to secondary school, perhaps by developing a particular relationship with one or more feeder primary schools and by assisting with work experience, links with industry and commerce, careers training and preparation for future employment and adult life.

With teachers and parents

- To foster the parents' understanding of the part they play in the social and educational development of their children.
- To use the skills and abilities of parents to the benefit of the child and the school.
- To help parents to become involved in the life of the school.
- To develop a parent/community room and resources, and to make the school more welcoming in spirit and appearance to parents and the community.
- To signal to parents and the wider community that all religions, cultures and languages are valued, respected and essential to the educational processes of the school.
- To help parents and the wider community to join with the school to celebrate various religious and culturally significant occasions.
- Where appropriate to open the school to evening, weekend and holiday use, and to seek assistance and appropriate funding and staffing.
- To develop home-visiting schemes and to help parents use relevant support agencies to eliminate impediments to the child's health and social and educational well-being.

With teachers within the community

- To open the school to community-based groups and to help such groups to form.
- To attend the functions of community groups and, where appropriate, help them to develop and achieve their aims, and to liaise effectively with relevant professional agencies.
- To explore ways of enabling more people within the community to gain the confidence and ambition to undertake further training and gain relevant qualifications and experience which raise their status.
- To assist with the development of educational activities of mutual benefit to the school and community.
- To liaise with community groups and officers from other departments to assist with the general development of the wider community.

With the head and administration/development officer

- To be a member of the school's senior management team and to help both head and team to enthuse the whole school with the new, community-sensitive approach of the school and to ensure that it is suffused throughout the school's development plan.

Both the head and the ICES will be particularly helped by the school's new administration and development officer. These three senior staff members are amongst those who will most clearly understand the direction in which the school is moving. Together, they will help all the staff to gradually appreciate the benefits to be gained from their new position. It will be appropriate to return to a further consideration of their task and how they can help their colleagues when the function of the community education enterprise centre is discussed in Chapter 10.

The ordinary teacher

Ordinary teachers will need close support in developing their skills in the classroom, particularly as their eyes might be diverted by the dangers inherent in SG schools and LM ones becoming associated respectively with Conservative and Labour thinking. There is a similar danger in the different kinds of intelligence, course content and teaching methods becoming typecast in a political context. Right-wing think-tanks could so associate 'cognitive' intelligence with 'subject' content and teaching by 'instruction' that teachers are frightened into thinking that the Government's reforms are intended to take us all back to Victorian times. Similarly, there is a danger that parents and Conservatives typecast teachers as being only interested in 'trendy' or 'project' work, 'interpersonal' intelligence and 'discovery' methods.

Irrespective of its source, such stereotyping would be unfortunate. Not only can it cloud understanding and cause unnecessarily hostile postures to be struck by the respective parties, but the subtlety of the teaching process can be obscured and the teacher undermined. It is important to look more closely at how the different components of the teaching/learning process interrelate.

Types of lesson content and teaching method

The distinction and relationship between 'project' and 'subject' work is not to be confused with the difference between so-called modern 'discovery' methods of teaching and more structured and 'traditional' ones. Project and subject work are two interdependent ways of presenting the content and quality of what is taught. Discovery and traditional styles of teaching are about the method of teaching and presenting the content. Just as the content of project and subject work are not opposites but complement and inform each other, so also discovery and traditional forms of teaching are compatible, but they are misnamed and often misunderstood.

Plato and Socrates taught by the supposedly 'modern' discovery method of asking questions which their students in ancient Greece had to answer for themselves. Like every good teacher who followed after them, they also knew when to tell their students what the answers were. Good, experienced teachers have always been able to organize their lessons in such a way that now one, now the other kind of method is used when it is appropriate. Indeed the more closely we look at the two different kinds of method the easier it is to recognize that there are rather more than two types. Professor Clem Adelman has pointed out that children of all ages learn in more than twenty ways. He groups them in four distinct types of method. Sally Tomlinson summarized these in a way which is instantly recognizable to most people:

1   *Instruction*: which can be lectures, whole-class instruction, drill or rote.
2   *Guided discovery*: this can take the form of question and answer, project work, simulation, role play or discussion or independent study.
3   *Guided inquiry*: this also can be question and answer, project work, simulation, role play, discussion or independent study.
4   *Pure inquiry*: this takes the form of independent study.

The best teachers have always used a blend of these four types of method, in conjunction with project and subject types of course content, in a way which they judge most appropriate for their pupils. Of course, there are many different possible blends. Each pupil and class of pupils relies heavily on their teacher to get the particular blend right at each step in the learning process. The blend will often vary according to which particular kind of intelligence is being addressed in pupils. Thus, one blend may be more appropriate at one stage for the development of cognitive intelligence while another blend may make sense for the development of interpersonal intelligence.

In this sense teaching is a long-established art and not an exact or developing science. It is acquired from the previous generation of expert teachers and practised afresh by each new generation of teachers. Unlike science, the art of teaching is much the same now as it was in the time of the ancient Greeks. There really is no one correct way to teach at any one moment, and there is no new, modern way which can improve on the tried and tested practices. All approaches have their proper time and place dependent upon the relationship and progress made between teacher and taught. This is why the teacher, like the craftsperson, needs to go through a structured and lengthy apprenticeship during which they learn by example and deed at the feet of those of proven ability. Some will become versatile in all approaches. Others will excel in one but not in another.

Only if the structure and content of a teacher's apprenticeship itself becomes too heavily biased in the direction of either project or subject work on the one hand and either discovery or traditional methods on the other do real problems arise. This is particularly so if the apprenticeship is so coloured by fashion or political trend or theory that project work and discovery teaching become artificially aligned and are held to be distinct from and incompatible with subject-oriented traditional teaching. This is what began to happen in the years leading up to the publication of the *Plowden Report* (1967). The report accelerated the trend and gave respectability to those who were arguing that discovery teaching and project work was *the* right way to teach and that subject and

traditional teaching methods were to be decried as old-fashioned. Now that the relatively universal application of this trend has been identified as being unhelpful to many
teachers and pupils, thus contributing towards poor standards, it is to be hoped that the
pendulum will not simply swing in the opposite direction for this would merely create
a different set of difficulties for other teachers and pupils.

Types of assessment

The dichotomy between 'traditional' and 'progressive' methods of teaching applies
to assessment of pupils' work. The point can be illustrated by reference to comments
by the staff of the English department and headteacher of Baverstock School. They
write:

> When our former students return to us, they delight in bouts of nostalgia regarding school
> expeditions, the old camaraderie, the eccentricities of their teachers and, now invariably,
> the academic fulfilment and positive attitudes to learning gained through their experience
> of coursework.
>
> Who would have believed that the 'class of '92', beset by the vaunted attractions of TV,
> videos, quadrophonic sound and computer graphics, would have developed better attitudes
> to learning than their predecessors who formed their negative views of schooling twenty
> to thirty years ago? Yet, the privileged few who then succeeded now wish to impose their
> perceived wisdom on the children of those who failed, without an appreciation of a method-
> ology which actually works for the great majority of pupils.
>
> The old 'cramming' system used in English not only involved regurgitating the teacher's
> notes with little real interaction with the text but it also restricted the amount of reading.
> Pupils could escape with reading fewer texts in a narrower range because of intensified
> study. It was common practice, for example, to read only one novel, one play and some
> poetry. Teachers spent so much time anticipating and preparing for every possible question
> that might be set that there was insufficient time left for other, more vital aspects of their
> English education.
>
> This forced the teacher/pupil partnership to collude in the learning of tricks for answer-
> ing questions rather than preparing a scenario for a genuine response. Therefore, candi-
> dates who were unlucky enough to have a teacher who failed to spot the question, or to
> have hay fever or suffer an illness on the day, did not enjoy similar opportunities to their
> modern counterparts whose reading is tailored to their particular stage of development. For
> them, more difficult tasks can be encouraged as appropriate.
>
> Not many realize that set texts are also ruinous to the school's capitation. English depart-
> ments all over the country still have 240 copies of *Lark Rise to Candleford* and *Lost World
> of the Kalahari* collecting dust on shelves, each chosen, then removed by a group of
> examiners, only to be replaced by 240 copies of some other text. Now that schools can
> manage their own scarce resources they are likely to urge a wiser way of investing them in
> developing the reading stock of a school to the best advantage of their children.
>
> Perhaps those who advocate examinations are concerned that the 'classics' might other-
> wise be neglected. Of course, the classics should be encouraged as pupils become ready for
> such work which is required for GCSE grades C and above and can be specifically built into
> the coursework syllabus. Good teachers know that there is a greater chance of turning
> pupils into readers for pleasure if there has been no switching off at the beginning of their
> life at school.
>
> Coursework provides constant motivation and positive feedback. It allows pride to arise
> from the development of work. It sets high standards from the start because all work is
> assessable. Examinations tell pupils that their day-to-day work does not 'count' in the same
> way. Therefore, they do not stretch themselves. Moreover, working on a pupil's weaknesses
> as they arise is hugely preferable to failure in an examination. Coursework allows weaker

pupils in particular to 'knock over' a grade at a time, to move from F to E and D in a steady, structured way because the targets set are visible and achievable. Sudden death examinations are remote with the target hopelessly beyond the confidence of many.

Whilst sample examination papers demoralize pupils from the start, coursework for the less able allows constant interaction with the teacher and other pupils. It provides structured support for their learning whereas examinations impose external demands which are not related to most pupils' skills and abilities. Unaided, many pupils cannot tackle examination papers. For example, in Baverstock about 70 per cent of the pupils fit into this category. Set-piece examinations can disadvantage and demotivate these pupils. They can fail in other ways in addition to the examinations. They risk seeing themselves and of being seen as 'dim' when they need as much praise and self-esteem as they can get.

The criteria for C to A grades look for abstract thought. Pupils in the D range and below are characterized by the fact that they still tend to think predominantly in concrete terms. They can peruse abstract questions but need guidance. Coursework allows for such assistance which then enables abstract thought to be reflected in the D to F mark. Assessment can help here in a way which exams cannot.

Coursework is appropriate for pupils of all abilities and the vast majority of pupils prefer it. Simply because able pupils can cope with examinations does not mean that they are a better means of assessing pupils. Coursework is a suitable preparation for advanced and higher education. It encourages independence and exploration – depth and diversity. It allows the pursuit of individual interests and thus enhances commitment, yet a comprehensive syllabus guards against narrowness. At the same time, coursework is more suitable for the less able. The skill levels, motivation and interest of Baverstock's share of these pupils have been maintained through coursework in a way which is inconceivable if examinations had been driving their education.

A major fear seems to be cheating in the form of additional help from home, but good teachers pick up on this easily. It is simple to monitor, but can also be praiseworthy and important. Children with difficulties need home help as well as fine teaching in school. Whatever system of assessment is used, some pupils will be advantaged because of their home background: pupils whose parents naturally converse with them; who provide cultural opportunities; who have books at home; who provide them with a rich environment; who, in other words, provide them with coursework at home. Little wonder that they are motivated and confident enough to do well in examinations. Coursework in school is not just of benefit to them, it also enables those who are starved of extensive support at home to begin to capture the point and joy of learning.
(*Phoenix Journal*, 1993)

While arguing against a wholesale return to the assessment style of yesterday, it is not suggested that coursework should now reign supreme to the exclusion of examinations. Rather, a balance must be struck which helps rather than hinders the teaching process. The best of both worlds is needed, not the dogmatic imposition of either.

The teachers in the SG school are no more or less sensitive to the needs of their pupils than their LM counterparts. Merely, they teach within the context of a culture which enables the organization of the educational input of the school to be in the control of the teachers and the head. Resources and skills are fully deployed at the chalk-face. It is then no longer incumbent on government to prescribe which way round to hold the chalk.

The roles of the head, ICES and administration/development officer

The roles of the head, ICES and administration/development officer include being the organizers of their school's resources. This role is crucial in helping teachers to

develop their skills and confidence. Acting as their school's 'teacher support service' they will provide both experienced and new teachers with support materials, staff and aims. More especially, they could provide the harassed and hard-working staff with a little more time away from the chalk-face in order to research and prepare the right blend of content and method and testing for the particular requirements of their individual pupils.

Not only the teacher, but the whole school can lose its way unless it is well and clearly led by confident senior managers. Hence, the purpose of a school's development plan, write Hargreaves and Hopkins (1991), is to:

> improve the quality of teaching and learning in a school through the successful management of innovation and change. Development planning encourages governors, heads and staff to ask and answer four basic questions:
> 'Where is the school now?
> What changes do we need to make?
> How shall we manage these changes over time?
> How shall we know whether our management of change has been successful?'
> Development planning helps the school to provide practical answers to these questions
> ... The gain is that the school is enabled to organize what it is already doing and what it needs to do in a more purposeful and coherent way

which makes sense to and includes all staff. Making the same point in a different way, in *Ten Good Schools*, HMI (1977) reported that the good school is one which can show:

> quality in its aims, in oversight of pupils, in curriculum design, in standards of teaching and academic achievements and in its links with the local community. [What all good schools have in common is] effective leadership and a climate (or culture) that is conducive to growth.
> (p. 36)

The emergence of a vision or a mission statement for the school and the organizational means of achieving it enables an ordinary school which understands its pupils to undergo the culture and attitude change which is required to become a good school.

Only those schools and teachers who believe in their own ability and produce visible, high-quality results will command the respect of the communities which they serve. A key feature of this self-belief relates to the teachers' expectations of their pupils. The art of teaching relies more on self-fulfilling prophecy and acts of will than on any scientific theory. Only those who have the character, reinforced by the atmosphere, structure and culture of the school, to insist that their pupils are able to reach beyond themselves, will find that they do so.

It is clear that the head must be the school's ultimate community education specialist and that the member of staff, if such there is, who carries the specialist post must at all times be seen by all other teachers to be acting for the head. One beneficial result which will flow from the increased status role of the ICES is that post-holders should be regarded as en route to becoming heads themselves. With the passage of time, this will ensure that most heads will be able to act as their school's ICES and ensure that community education suffuses their school's development plan and culture.

REFERENCES

Hargreaves, D. and Hopkins, D. (1991) *The Empowered School*. London: Cassell.
HMI (1977) *Ten Good Schools*. London: DES.
Phoenix Journal (1993) Moseley, Birmingham: Phoenix Centre.
Plowden, Lady (1967) *Children and Their Primary School*. London: HMSO.

Chapter 10

Clusters of Neighbouring Schools

Before LM was introduced following the 1988 education legislation, heads and governors had only been accustomed to handling the small change of their school fund. Independence means that the typical primary school head will have to manage a budget of £700,000, while a secondary school head could have a figure of £2,000,000 or more to contend with. Running a school as a business with a large turnover as well as managing a successful educational enterprise can be daunting, if not frightening. It requires the acumen of a business manager with risk-taking skills as well as the vision of a good teacher. We have already considered that while the bold might take the decision to leave the LEA in their stride, many others will hesitate.

The appointment of an ICES and an administration/development officer will help. So will training, but another powerful factor is contained in the possibility of small groups of neighbouring schools, particularly primary schools, clustering together and, perhaps, becoming self-governing at the same time. Under LEA management, schools tended not to have very much to do with each other as each related separately to the town hall. Once under the management of the community they will need to explore ways of supporting one another. Most of the many neighbourhoods which make up each town contain several primary schools and perhaps one secondary school which is likely to draw a significant proportion of its pupils from these feeder primaries. Typically, let us say, a cluster of ten such schools might include nine primaries and one secondary. Problems and possibilities, physical resources and equipment can readily be shared between them.

Not all schools are likely to wish to develop a fully-fledged dual-use policy. Most will wish to deepen their relationship with parents which can often be done in the school day with only modest evening commitments. Few will have the resources to open their buildings from 7.30 a.m. to 10.00 p.m. for fifty weeks a year, nor is it necessary to do so to convey the right welcoming and parent-involving signals.

Within each neighbourhood perhaps just one or two schools will develop the full range of community school activities. The others will wish to specialize in other, equally vital pursuits. For example, one of the ten schools may wish to develop its scientific pursuits. As with dual use, not all schools will either have the aptitude, funds or facilities to take on the full range of scientific interests which the national curriculum invites. One

school, however, might argue that its 'pets corner' could be developed into a farm so that animal husbandry and market gardening, as well as science, are added to its curriculum and school prospectus. However, it will wish to share these resources and the skills of its staff with its neighbouring schools, for in turn, it will want to use those of their facilities which are in advance of its own.

Another school might have particularly attractive playing fields and a keen sporting interest. It might become a focal point of good practice in music, movement, physical education, games and keep-fit classes for older people in the area. Each neighbourhood school may develop its own special strength and interest. Not only would this begin to provide parents with something of a real rather than an artificial choice, but it would enable the schools themselves to tap into and reinforce each other's special skills and resources.

Such a set of interrelated schools within their own community might reach beyond the stage of seeing themselves as ten separate, attractive, welcoming but different schools, each with their own individual prospectus, magazine and teachers. They could become like federal units within a wider neighbourhood cluster. Once seen in this interdependent light, it is a short step for these proudly separate but interdependent parts of a whole community education network to produce their own attractive group brochure. 'Come to our neighbourhood.' 'Send your child to our cluster.' 'Come to teach in our network, we have ten schools, all vibrant and challenging, look at our facilities, look at the support and training we give you.' It is an interesting way forward in these days of teacher shortages. Those whom the LEA could not attract may be more open to a 'small is beautiful' offer from a group of enthusiastic heads and governors. Of course, as soon as one set of schools starts to act in this way it will become incumbent on others to follow suit for fear of being left behind.

The clinching argument which clusters of schools might use to sell themselves could be the offer of subsidized accommodation for the first year of the diffident probationer's working life. Each neighbourhood has its row of derelict terraced houses or its high-rise block of flats which is shunned by the elderly and those with families. Why not convert such a property to attract young teachers to live in the area in which they are being invited to teach? Such accommodation would provide a protected, supportive and thoughtful transition from the sheltered college dormitory to the world of adult work. Similarly, one of the neighbourhood's ten schools might open a privately-run, extended day nursery and latch-key provision for the married teacher with a child or two who otherwise could not yet return to teaching.

It only takes one further step for the cluster to realize that it could jointly act as its own teacher-training college. It could thus offer a hands-on transition from training through probation to the status of a fully-fledged teacher, a real apprenticeship in a real work context. The head and mature staff will wish to pay close attention to the nature of the induction which the new teacher receives in their first school. For, during this period, the newcomer is often left largely to his or her own devices. Hard-pressed and experienced teachers do not always have the time to supervise the apprentice to their own satisfaction let alone to that of anyone else. Consequently, only the transparently bad teacher is encouraged to leave the profession. Yet many more young teachers need further help and guidance if they are to succeed. It is because they do not always receive this support that large numbers of expensively-trained teachers leave the profession unnecessarily.

Proper supervision by a teacher mentor would enhance each cluster's ability to care properly for the young teacher, to visit them in their sheltered accommodation, offer extra guidance and familiarize them with the community.

It should be possible for good school managers to provide first and second-year teachers with at least one day a week away from pupil contact. This would enable them to study and reflect on their teaching experience, visit other schools, shops and industry, and prepare their own project and community work. Furthermore, it should be possible to reward experienced teachers with the necessary time away from their classes so that they can pass on their expertise to new teachers and further develop their own special interests. The communal space in each set of apprentice teachers' flats could quickly become the treasured in-service teacher support centre for each cluster. It could become the focal point for the development of new ideas and projects as well as for mutual support. It might, for example, become the curriculum and timetable planning centre in which the ideas are first generated which lead to a shift system enabling interested teachers to take, say, a morning off to enable them to organize an evening project activity for pupils and parents, or where a local industrialist discusses the secondment of a colleague to the classroom to help pupils to work on a project while the class teacher gains a little experience in the factory.

Finance

At first glance the finance needed to underpin such developments might seem beyond the reach of an ordinary school. Before the advent of LM and SG, schools did not see or know anything of their school's finances. They did not know how its budget was allocated and spent. Was their school solvent? Was it bankrupt? Did it have a surplus? Not only did the school not know the answer to these questions, neither did the LEA. Self-government offers schools the prospect of receiving the LEA's retained percentage of their budget (15 per cent or less). If the cluster of ten schools was to share only 10 per cent of these sums then a substantial amount becomes available each year for imaginative, new use. The sums might be as follows:

Budgeting gains made by SG schools over LM schools

	SG	LM (SG – 15%)	Gain
Secondary	£2,000,000	£1,700,000	£300,000
Primary	£700,000	£595,000	£105,000

The total gain of 10 schools (1 secondary, 9 primary) is thus:
£300,000 + £105,000 × 9 = £1,245,000.
Just 10 per cent of this gain = £124,500.

The most obvious joint appointment for a do-it-yourself cluster to make first from this sum might be an administration/development officer. Indeed, as pointed out earlier, the appointment might be made even before the schools have become indepen-dent, for the post-holder will be an invaluable help in easing each school from one status to the other.

Perhaps the second most obvious use of a pooled budget might be to appoint one or two extra teachers to be shared between the cluster of schools. Schools, especially primaries, may not have sufficient finance to appoint their own ICES but each could benefit from the support of one or two shared posts. Exactly the same point relates to other potential support posts, such as education social workers, language development, science, music, physical education and other specialists. Each cluster, then, could readily develop its own quality support team (QST) which might either be based in an empty teaching room in the cluster's leading school or dispersed throughout the cluster. The 'ordinary' teacher who feels anxious when confronted by the community education-oriented national curriculum may feel that the QST is like the Seventh Cavalry appearing on the hill. A cluster of schools' own tailor-made QST can be invaluable to both new and experienced teachers alike.

Community education enterprise centre

Alongside the quality support team of professional staff an equally significant small team can be envisaged, the practical support team (PST). Previously, the LEA and city direct labour force had become quite incapable of maintaining and developing school buildings and sites. The school's paint was peeling. The school sign had warped and collapsed. The entrance way looked more like a closed off and disused exit than a point of welcome. The school field and hedge was overgrown and the boundary fence was strewn with litter. Inside, the school looked no better. The last coat of paint in each classroom must have been thinly administered over walls, door, drawing pins and sticky tape a decade ago. The effect which all this cumulatively created was one of neglect and lack of care – just the same effect as was engendered and reinforced by the poor quality of the surrounding environment. The message which this inadvertently conveyed to pupil, parent, teacher and community alike had become wholly negative.

In place of this state of affairs a small team of handymen, not unlike those administered by the new officer in Nicholas Chamberlaine School, could offer a cheap, practical alternative whereby the grounds are regularly maintained with pride. Horti-culturalists, painters and decorators, carpenters and brickies – the scope is so endless that, on the one hand, the potential for transforming the school's environment almost at a stroke can be envisaged while, on the other, the feat can be accomplished by setting up a series of small businesses which offer hands-on, educationally relevant training experiences. Whilst the PST could be initially subsidized from the new-found shared finances of the cluster of schools, it could be sustained long term from within each school's own maintenance budget. The team would be driven to succeed by providing the services which the schools need, when they need them, at the quality and price they demand.

At least one of the cluster of ten schools is likely to have the space to accommodate both the QST and PST. The base for both teams might be sensibly termed a community education and enterprise centre (CEEC). Each CEEC would be capable of offering the following range of services:

To schools – practical (PST)

- Grounds maintenance
- Painting and decorating
- Production of resource materials
- Small building works
- Catering
- Cleaning and caretaking
- Printing

To schools – professional (QST)

- Development
- Fund-raising and applications to government
- Bursar as administrative officer
- Teacher support services
- Teacher recruitment and accommodation
- Image and presentation
- Community events
- Training for parents and pupils on placement to the CEEC

To the community (PST and QST)

- Graffiti removal
- Employment training and small business creation
- Production of a community newspaper
- Maintenance of 'confused' derelict sites
- Maintenance of small parks and roads

Each CEEC could be run either by one of the cluster of ten schools or it could be set up as an independent limited company and charity on whose board sit representatives from each school and the community. The possibility of the CEEC becoming a free-standing community business and trust which enhances both the schools and the general environment is real. Its broader purpose might be the regeneration of community purpose, ambition, vision, and capacity for action. Figure 10.1 shows a picture of each city's education system before and after SG schools were created.

In 1970 St Paul's in Balsall Heath began to devise a number of support services, which were managed by people drawn from the local community. These services were of value first for the community, then for the nearby group of a dozen schools. Development was hard, for the project started with £50 and a great deal of purely voluntary effort. The definition and perception of its activities and aims were that they were quite peripheral to the mainstream of social and educational life. Nevertheless it painfully constructed a nursery centre, resource centre and farm, a language development and

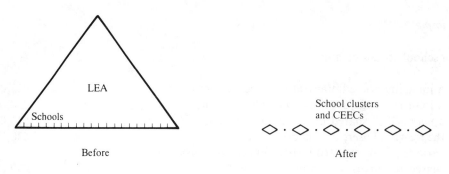

Figure 10.1 *Style of co-operation before and after self-government.*

support project, school, newspaper, printing facility and education enterprise centre. It opened its buildings and grounds to become the village hall and village green of the area. Whilst it flourished independently, it could not easily see how its support services could be duplicated and financed elsewhere.

Today any school or cluster of schools could sponsor and subsidize such activities. Any schools wishing to do so will, of course, stamp their own particular needs and interests upon the institutions which they devise. Their quality support team might help their farm to identify and develop an interest in science and technology while their PST could build the farm. Their language development project and theatre may signal their special concern with English, other languages and the performing arts.

It would even be possible to duplicate St Paul's school for children with difficulties. For the White Paper of 1992 and Bill of 1993 opened the way for groups of parents and teachers to start their own SG school from scratch with a grant from the Department for Education. It will be interesting to see whether several clusters of schools, each with its own secondary school, might together set up their own St Paul's-like school for children who find it difficult to attend and behave in the large school setting.

Irrespective of the diverse and special interests which a cluster of schools might develop with the help of their quality and practical support teams, their practical community education enterprise centre might not only help their buildings to appear attractive and cared for but also assist with the development of their community, even becoming its 'dynamo' for recovery and the focus of 'village' life.

At last it becomes possible to see how the St Paul's 'experiment' can be duplicated in spirit and style, if not in detail, in a range of areas in each city. It is not necessary to find extra finance to fund a complicated range of community-run services and institutions. The necessary money can be found by redistributing finance from the city centre out to schools. It can then be used by individual schools and clusters of schools in imaginative and constructive ways to provide themselves and their neighbourhood with their own particular needs.

To demonstrate that schools can do far more by linking together in fresh ways than by going it alone perhaps two modest examples are in order:

Example 1

Ten schools could create:

• a joint finance/administrative/development officer	£22,000
• a joint language development or TIE teacher	£20,000
• a network of shared in-service support courses	£13,000
• their own adviser, pre-school workers or various part-timers from special needs to music	£30,000
• shared resources – van – printing and publicity – painting and decorating	£39,500

TOTAL   £124,500

Staff from a group of ten schools in Oxfordshire meet regularly to discuss the management of learning and behaviour. Teacher exchanges between the secondary and primary schools are frequent. Curricular strengths and weaknesses are targeted. Joint working groups exist in PE, CDT and English. New departures will presently include joint curriculum groups in all subject areas, partnership purchasing, and joint school meals and ground maintenance contracts.

Example 2

Ten schools could create:

• a finance/administrative/development officer	£22,000
• resourcing meetings for staff of ten schools	£2,000
• teacher exchange, materials	£1,000
• working groups	£1,000
• part-time specialists –11@£6,000 each	£66,000
• community education specialist	£22,000
• termly cluster, home/school, curriculum newsletter	£5,000
• annual cluster teacher recruitment and marketing brochure with conference	£5,500

TOTAL   £124,500

Each school and set of schools will, of course, have different priorities and needs. So, in order to answer these needs with its own DIY services, each area's joint cluster support system will be unique.

Rather than trying to do everything at once, a school or set of schools may wish to start with a competent finance/administrative/development officer to help build slowly and by degrees towards more ambitious targets. Indeed, even before a cluster is formed, a secondary school might lend its feeder primaries its new finance/administrative/development officer. This new type of post should enable a set of schools to:

- save the finance for the post within a year by careful planning;
- undertake joint supply and purchasing as a part of this planning process;
- gradually increase and manage the range and quality of shared support staff and resources for its teachers;
- gain a greater sense of common purpose, mutual support and high morale;
- take the strain from heads and senior managers;
- develop a cluster before considering moving together towards self-governing status.

The devolution of finance and control to LM and SG schools gives them the responsibility to manage their own affairs. This responsibility can only be exercised effectively if the administrative role which was locked within the central bureaucracy is relocated in schools and clusters of schools.

The new administration and development post advocated above could enable clusters of neighbouring schools to build their own 'cluster development plan' of pooled support services and resources to enhance each individual school's own plan. These cluster plans might include a programme for any or all of the areas shown in Figure 10.2.

Some schools in each town will continue to wish to stand on their own while others will cluster together and develop plans and activities as described above, but both will develop their own expertise and special interests which act as a magnet to others. These can be marketed thus making links which spread good practice, not only city wide, but between cities. These co-operative links will follow local lines of real interest and practical need. They will be unencumbered with costly and time-consuming administrative offices. Once diffident 'ordinary' teachers have experienced the supportive benefits of their CEEC and seen their neighbouring schools acting in concert rather than in competition then they are more likely to recognize the merits of self-government. Figure 10.3 shows the new links that might develop between schools.

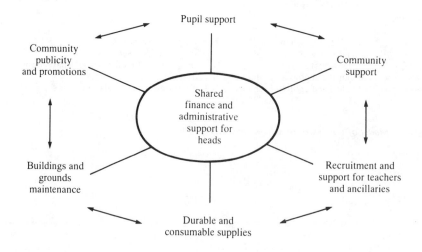

Figure 10.2   *A cluster development plan.*

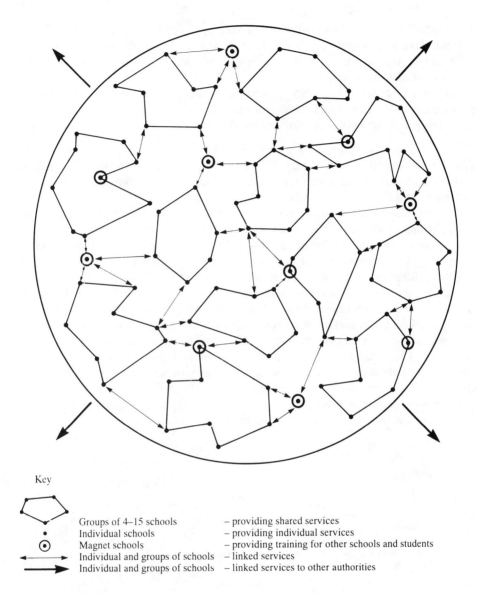

Key

Groups of 4–15 schools   – providing shared services
Individual schools   – providing individual services
Magnet schools   – providing training for other schools and students
Individual and groups of schools – linked services
Individual and groups of schools – linked services to other authorities

Figure 10.3   *Model of a network of schools in a city.*

Part 3

Refocusing Local Government and Political Theory

Now that the radical nature of self-governing schools has been outlined it is necessary to consider the implications for local authorities. Because they are losing control of their schools, does this mean that local government is weakened or does it present it with new opportunities? What are the implications of the SG school and clusters of schools for the community in which they are situated? The answers to these questions suggest that profound, but exciting, opportunities are opening for communities and local government. If confronted boldly, these opportunities can be fashioned into a key which opens the doors to the reconstruction of Britain's fading urban areas.

If the old school and LEA were related to the needs and culture of industrial society do the new SG school and clusters of schools relate to a post-industrial society? If so, what are the implications for the political process, political priorities and the way they shape policy?

Chapter 11

A New Authority for New Schools and Town Halls

Before discussing what kind of agencies, if any, might replace LEAs it is sensible to check that the confident new SG school really does leave the LEA without a role and that the prospect of its abolition is not a consequence of one-sided Conservative dogma. So, what were the key functions of LEAs and who now performs them?[1]

- It is now clear that LM and SG schools are taking from LEAs the major functions of finance, management, administration and control of the education process.
- The responsibility for further and higher education has already passed from the LEAs to colleges.
- In many authorities adult education is dealt with by departments other than the LEA such as leisure services departments.
- The inspection of schools is now independent and open to tender and competition. The best LEA and HMI professionals are forming new, independent teams of inspectors.
- Education welfare officers (EWOs) and educational psychologists, or the finance to fund or buy them as required, could easily and effectively be devolved to schools.
- School meals, cleaning, caretaking and a range of other services are also most effectively devolved out to schools or clusters of neighbouring schools.
- A range of new businesses is arising and existing ones are expanding to take in functions which the LEA once performed. Services ranging from grounds maintenance and payroll to the supply of teachers and advice on every aspect of the national curriculum are on offer at more competitive rates than most LEAs can muster.
- The careers service might be more appropriately dealt with by departments of economic development or the TEC. This would result in careers advice being based on the practical opportunities being offered in the real economy.
- Decisions about the number of school places and the opening of new schools will soon be shared between the LEA and the new funding agency when more than 10 per cent of either primary or secondary schools have become GM. Once 75 per cent have become GM the LEA will cease to have even this role.

- Even if a few residual functions which some schools need were retained by the local authority, such as legal advice, this does not require the existence of an LEA. Such functions can be performed in other quarters of the local authority.

On examination, it seems that there is nothing which the LEA has done in the past which in the future cannot be done more effectively by one or other of the following:

- SG schools themselves or clusters of schools.
- New, independent service deliverers.
- Other departments of the town hall.
- The new Department for Education's funding agency.

Once the LEA has gone the following consequences will become clear:

- The new school and the community will gain experience in management skills and the pride which comes from ownership.
- All available resources and teachers will be redistributed into the classroom.
- The town hall will be freed to undertake new, more achievable tasks.

However, before we finally accept that for all practical reasons the LEA really has become redundant we must ask if a democratic, local government role remains for it to play in broad principle. If so, we might yet be persuaded to keep it in existence. Certainly, those with an interest in its preservation say that the development of new schools removes power from the town hall and vests it in Whitehall. However, whilst central government has taken the lead in initiating change, most of the authority which is being removed from the LEAs has not passed to Whitehall but to the schools themselves.

In place of twenty or so politically-motivated councillors, sitting on the education committee which controls all the schools within the LEA, there are fifteen locally-elected parents and community representatives for each school. These governors have a passionate interest in the education which takes place within their particular school and not in politics in general. If there are, say, 200 schools in an LEA this means that 200 × 15 (3,000) local people are now involved who have a direct interest in the schools and not just a political interest. This significantly increases the level of participation and democracy. It makes schools much more, not less, accountable to local people. It also takes schools out of the party political arena where councillors live and firmly places them within the community where the children live.

It is important to look in turn at the new agencies which will gradually take the place of the LEA; first, the governing body of each school; second, independent suppliers; third, a new association for schools; fourth, a reformed town hall.

THE GOVERNING BODY

The vital, new, active citizen role of each school's governing body has already been discussed. Here, it is sufficient to recall that the LEA's old role is almost entirely split up into as many component parts as there are schools in its area. These parts are then devolved to those schools themselves. In effect, each independent school becomes its

own LEA. Indeed, some schools will require no separate authority distinct from or additional to that vested in their governing body, headteachers and staff.

INDEPENDENT SUPPLIERS

Any additional services which schools require, but which they cannot provide for themselves, individually or in clusters, will simply be bought in from independent commercial suppliers at a cheaper and more effective rate than could be supplied by the LEA. Existing businesses have extended their range of services and new businesses are arising which provide all the help which schools could wish for.

SCHOOLS EDUCATIONAL ASSOCIATIONS

Many schools which are on the brink of seeking independence hesitate because each school cares about other schools and not just themselves. They would not like to replace the LEA with an alternative step into the unknown which might spell isolation from other schools or a Hobbesian war of all against all in some purely competitive educational marketplace.

So far, each school's governors and parents have felt that they must make a decision about independence in terms of the specific interests of their own school. However, many also cast an eye to the wider good and wonder what might happen on a regional basis. Neither the Government nor anyone else has yet detailed what, if anything, it envisages the education system might look like after many schools have become self-governing. Schools wonder if there is a hidden agenda.

The Government made mistakes in 1988 and 1992 by merely opening the gate to independence without laying down a clear and socially coherent path which it expected everyone to tread towards a specified destination. Schools would like someone to explain the path and the destination right away. The required lead could come from Government or it could come from an enterprising group of schools or a town hall.

Whoever fills this gap and points to a harmonious and imaginative new way forward will perform an important service and, perhaps, influence the Government and the rest of the country. In practice, the rationale for any new, area-wide educational function and agency will not arise from the terminal need or interest of the old town hall educational supplier, but from the new customer, the new SG schools themselves or the schools which are about to become independent. The question is not whether these schools will wish to relate to each other in the absence of the LEA, but *how* they will wish to do it.

Schools will compare notes about who are the best independent suppliers, how clusters of schools can most benefit from CEECs and which QST and PST services are most effectively provided by themselves. Each school and cluster will eagerly seek examples of good practice in various subject areas. They will thirst for new and better methods of organizing their staff development programmes. As they talk about such matters they will discover new and better ways of relating to each other on an individual school-to-school and cluster-to-cluster basis. Much of this dialogue will be local, but some will take place over the same territory the LEA once covered and even beyond.

If there is to be a new, school-led agency beyond a variety of overlapping clusters it might be called the schools educational association (SEA) trust. The SEA trust might develop the following functions:

- An educational think-tank
- Quality advisers in special subject areas to disseminate good practice
- A collective shop window and advocate to both local and central government
- Publications
- Fund-raising and marketing of SEA trust initiatives

If each school in a city with, say, 200 schools contributed just 0.1 per cent of its annual budget to its SEA trust this would generate a sum of £200,000. This would easily cover the salary of twelve staff and the running costs. The staff could all be based in centres in schools, including those few in the 'shop window.' There is no need at all for them to be in an office somewhere in the city as they service schools, not the town hall.

The SEA trust could be responsible to a few teachers and governors elected from schools and clusters. They would employ the staff – largely teachers and heads – many of whom would be seconded from schools for periods of one to three years. There would be no need for a chief education officer (CEO) or administrators or managers, for these roles would have disappeared with the old LEA.

Almost all schools would subscribe to their area's SEA trust. To retain credibility and integrity it is important that the SEA trust is not in the control of local or central government but is clearly the employed agent of the schools. It would thus be able to represent schools to the town hall on a variety of issues from directly educational ones, such as special needs, to broader ones, such as the quality of life in the communities in which their children live.

It is equally important for the SEA trust to represent schools to the central government or its regional agencies. The Government needs to be told in no uncertain terms that some of the measures it takes are inadequate, not least the way it has presented the case for SG schools. The Conservative Governments of the 1980s and 1990s ran the risk of tarnishing the virtues of self-government with the idiosyncrasies of right-wing think-tanks on a wide range of issues. The present and any future enabling Government should value a series of regional practitioner's SEA trusts which could give strong advice about which reforms were working, which ones should be abandoned and which new ones ought to be put in place. Slim, cheap and directly representative of schools, SEA trusts are potentially far more important and effective bodies than the Government's own regional funding agencies. Indeed, SEA trusts suggest that the funding agencies are not necessary.

A NEW TOWN HALL

Many authorities have already discovered the benefits of devolving several of their noneducational services to the grass roots. The idea of the devolved neighbourhood office holds many attractions. It is time that the town hall's thinking about education caught up with that of other departments and that governors and local people were trusted both with the priceless asset of schools and the means of constructing their own ways of helping each other. We noted in Chapter 6 that some local authorities were

beginning to accept that their LEAs were likely to disappear. These authorities are beginning to grasp the nettle by devolving the whole of their education budget to schools, dissolving their education committees, cutting down on the number of their city departments and encouraging brand new ones to take their place.

Positive action of this kind by town halls would remove many of the lingering doubts which schools and local councillors might have about the virtues of self-government. It would also create an interesting new possibility for local government. Instead of retreating defensively before the legislation of the central government it could be turned to positive advantage. LEAs have long since ceased to fulfil any positive, developmental purpose and generate only grumbles and ill will, even from those who still argue for their retention. They consume large sums of money, councillors' time and produce only a bad image. The town hall can well do without this image, which conjures up only disrespect and gives local government a bad name.

It has long been accepted in the economic sphere that the only practical task which either central of local government can perform is to help to create a lively and stimulating context in which independent enterprise can flourish. The time has come when we must see educational authorities in the same light. There really are no tablets of stone which suggest that education must be run by town halls forever as if it were the one sacrosanct nationalized monopoly which could be retained from Britain's industrial past. Socialists and Conservatives alike must accept that this form of collective planning has passed its sell-by date. It has become a brake upon, not a stimulus for, progress in both schools and the town hall.

Once freed from their old tasks, both the town hall's and the councillors' time and energy could be allocated to tackling precisely those global responsibilities which neither schools nor their SEA trusts can undertake. These might include:

- ensuring that the transition from LM to SG is undertaken smoothly and that independence and entry into a new partnership of equals is freely given and does not have to be fought for;
- ensuring that someone provides for the needs of the underachieving school and enables it to flourish or closes it down;
- ensuring that someone attends to the special needs of the developing child at every level of its life whether in the family, the community or the school;
- stimulating and enabling the community as a whole to become spirited and revitalized;
- setting a local agenda and targets for the city or region to adopt and aim for which are idealistic, compelling and challenging enough to inspire a whole variety of SG schools, businesses and voluntary agencies.

As with the SEA trust, if each school voluntarily contributed just 0.1 per cent of its budget (making a total of 0.2 per cent) then an area covered by 200 schools would generate £200,000. This would readily pay for the 'educational' input of the town hall's new department.

When they are established, these new 'children's and community' departments will liaise with both schools, SEA trusts and other local and business agencies.

SG schools, clusters of schools and their SEA trusts will happily look after the task of educating their children with the help of services which they can buy in from independent suppliers. Clusters of schools will even be able to suggest and enhance a weak

neighbour more effectively than any other authority. However, they cannot ensure that either the family or community in which their children live is spirited and pulling in the same direction as the school and its teachers. Without a partnership between school, home and community, even the best school will fail. Just as schools need confident local authorities to enable them to mature and become self-governing, so they also need strong, visionary local authorities to support and enable families and communities to become self-reliant. Schools and their SEA trust have much to discuss with and expect from their local authority. For this reason it is unwise to suggest that SG schools want to 'opt out' from the local authority and be 'independent' of it. Rather, they want to opt into a new, more mature partnership.

It is particularly difficult to see why the central government's proposed funding agencies are necessary. They, and not SG schools, smack of a right-wing central government attack upon urban authorities. There is no obvious task which they could perform which could not be undertaken by a computer in the town hall or by a continuation of the SEA trust and the local authority's new children's and community department. Sensible SG schools and SEA trusts will oppose them. Sensible government would take the point. It is now possible to complete the models first illustrated in Chapter 6 (see Figure 11.1).

AGENTS OF CHANGE

The LEA monopoly over state education is in the process of being replaced by a number of different agencies: schools and their governing bodies; independent suppliers of services; SEA trusts; and new types of local authorities. Far from diminishing local democracy these developments enhance and improve it by freeing town halls from the task of managing schools and enabling them to concentrate on fresh, more appropriate tasks. However, the process of change from the pyramid-like LEA to a new state of affairs will take several years to work through the system as schools, local communities and town halls adjust and react to the various opportunities which face them. Until the dust of change has settled down it is not possible to foresee exactly what the final outcome might be. There is no guarantee that it will take the form outlined in these pages.

It could be that either traditional Labour or Conservative dogma will win the day. If unreconstructed Labour LEAs succeed in halting the process of reform then a two-tier system of LM and SG schools could arise. If, as a result of entreaties by the Conservative Government, more and more schools simply go SG without any means of mutual co-operation, then competitition and anarchy could result. Either way, schools and the overall provision of education will be unsatisfactory. The Government will be criticized for starting the process of reform in the first place without properly completing it and the radical potential of self-government will have been lost.

How can these unsatisfactory outcomes be avoided? Who is powerful enough to ensure that the radical option prevails? Perhaps the Government could change its stance and encourage LEAs to pursue the harmonious, co-operative route to independence. The town halls could move from defence to offence and set the pace themselves. Or, central and local government could combine to help schools to take the harmonious road forward. Unfortunately these possibilities have not so far been adopted. There is, however, another possibility which could prove decisive.

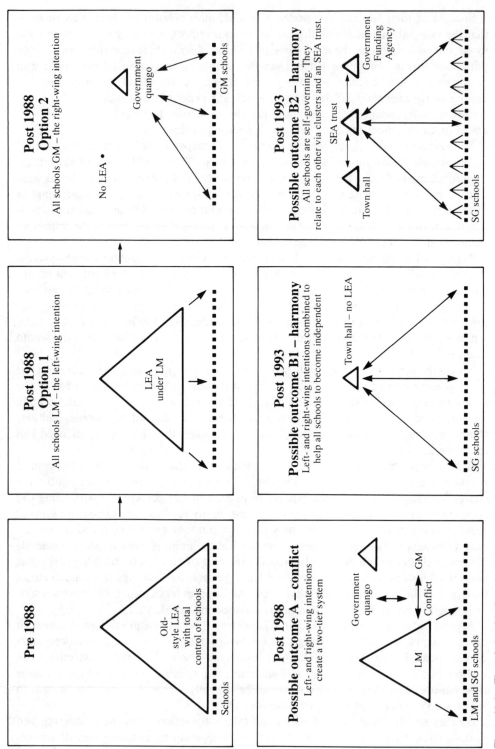

Figure 11.1 *The relationship between LM and SG schools, local authorities and government.*

Because of their successful experience of LM, most schools are beginning to sense that the tide has turned. Once dependent upon a remote authority to tell them what to do and how to do it, the experience of LM has shown them that they can now do things for themselves rather better than this authority can. Whilst some could wait no longer and have become SG, many more are now champing at the bit as they too desire control over their affairs. They are now the experts in and pioneers of the new culture of independence. They are not only ahead of town hall thinking, they are also ahead of Government policy. They are in a strong position.

The next set of LM schools which contemplates independence may, therefore, reflect before simply following the SG route on their own. They could view the advantages of autonomy as of value not just for their own school but for their neighbours as well. They might see the benefit in moving towards self-government at the same time as their neighbours. Perhaps a cluster of schools might consider self-government in conjunction with each other or, more imaginatively, most or all of the schools within an authority might seek self-government together.

Acting rather like an SEA trust before one has been formed, schools might present their town hall with a proposal: 'Don't give us 85 per cent or even 95 per cent of our budgets. We want full autonomy to manage our affairs. We intend to set up our own SEA trust, preferably with your blessing. This gives you the chance of reforming your town hall and making it more responsive to the needs of the 1990s. You can then form a new enabling partnership with us.' This could be an offer which town halls would find difficult to refuse.

No doubt most city fathers will instinctively want to negotiate some compromise which preserves some role for the LEA. Yet, if schools hold firm to their vision of the future there is nothing the town hall could do. Schools really are now in the driving seat provided they can make the intellectual break with the old dependency culture. Can schools muster the courage to tell their old manager that the tide has changed and that they are now in charge?

If the city fathers turn down this offer, then all the schools have to do is to begin to pursue the route to independence collectively. Those who argue for the status quo often charge individual schools which express an interest in self-government with being too competitive or self-seeking. This charge is most easily refuted if neighbouring schools move towards self-government at the same time and take every step together. So far, only a few sets of two schools have done this but the point is more impressively made if a whole cluster of schools or all schools in the area of an LEA do so. There are other gains if schools proceed in this way, not least the fact that it brings them much closer together. It helps them realize that they can support each other in various ways, including the creation of shared support services and an SEA trust.

A good, informed, co-ordinated vote is not only likely to ensure self-government, it could also give each school a flying start on the upward curve of their own independent development. It can serve to unite and invigorate a school. If these collective steps which schools could take towards self-government are spelled out in advance, it makes it even more likely that most town halls will eventually accept the inevitable, accede to the schools' request and voluntarily dissolve their LEA.

As they slowly disappear, LEAs should take satisfaction from the pioneering and positive contribution they have made to the development of a state system of schools for all. They should also note that the infant, dependent schools which they created and

cared for are now coming of age, gaining maturity and clamouring for independence. It is good that thousands of parents and community figures are now prepared to take on the task of running these schools which the LEA once undertook for them. Indeed, it is not just good for schools, it is also a sign of strong, developing communities and of an enlightened, confident town hall. It is time to look at the urban communities in which most schools are situated and spell out the implications of SG schools for the further reform of local government and the devolution of central control to neighbourhoods.

NOTE

1. This list of functions was first suggested to the author by Bryan Stoten.

Chapter 12

The Urban Village

It is clear that one reason why so very many residents in Balsall Heath, Druids Heath, Small Heath and the inner and outer ring areas of each urban sprawl are alienated from and careless about their fellow citizens is because their own neighbourhood has lost its identity. It became encompassed within and its boundaries obliterated by the urban expanse of Birmingham, Leeds or London which is too large to identify with. Modern cities cannot take the place of the extended family, the street and smaller village of yesteryear from which people gained their first sense of place, security, familiarity and personal identity.

Similarly, as the city has grown, so too have many invisible, intangible city-wide services which aim to be 'provided for' the resident by planning experts (the 20 per cent) who are trained to 'know' what people want. Nothing is asked from ordinary residents (the 80 per cent) in return, no active part is held out for them to play in their own community.

Residents can see what is wrong with their streets, buildings, open spaces and schools and in the lack of employment which surround them – and are accordingly depressed. Hitherto, however, they have not felt able or seen how to put things right – and have thus become undervalued. What can be done *with* residents? What contribution can they make to their community, to provide it with the spirit with which they can identify?

First, residents can help to diagnose problems. Ordinary people are concerned not just by poor standards in education, but also by:

- The dirt, litter and rubbish which confront them everywhere.
- The rise in crime, the fact that they do not feel safe or secure in their own home and cannot leave their back doors open, let alone be able to walk the streets at night.
- The high incidence of family breakdown.
- The lack of proportion or grace in modern buildings.
- Their own unfulfilled need to express care and concern, and to do something to improve their circumstances, including via real employment.

Second, residents can begin to define themselves into the solution of these problems. There is a Good Samaritan in everyone regardless of circumstance. Very many people

give to 'Children in Need' and 'Comic Relief'. Everyone is touched by Princess Anne's Presidency of Save the Children and Prince Charles' concern with the grotesque architecture which has come to blight city life.

Despite much talk of the power of the active or caring citizen, local and central government have yet to recognize or tap his hidden reserves and apply them where charity really belongs, in the local community – in the urban village. Whoever does tap these reserves will connect with a powerful, subterranean characteristic in the make-up of every citizen. Given its head, this characteristic could become an unstoppable force for good.

Most ordinary people recognize, indeed applaud, the role the State or city must play in upholding access for all to basic human needs and the fundamental requirements of a civilized society. Most thus recognize the enforced giving of taxes to ensure these support services are available for all. But most ordinary people also recognize that individuals have a part to play in actively seeking to improve their own lives. They know they must take part in securing their own health, and in being a participant in their own and their child's education and in the provision of a secure environment for their families. In order to do this, the individual must also play a part in helping others to build up a wider community which provides all with leisure pursuits, a pleasant environment, festive occasions and religion. In other words, the individual helps to create an enterprising, self-help community. The fabric of society does not have an independent existence of its own. It is sustained, created and developed by the individual. The individual's contributions make it what it is – for ill or good. Far too long ignored, that contribution must now be recognized and enhanced through the structures by which society is governed.

St Paul's Project raises £70,000 every year from Balsall Heath. It gives people pride and a purpose to know that they are not pawns in an all-powerful State which leaves no place for the individual. They like to receive help when and where they are weak, provided they can and are encouraged to give where they are strong. It is important not to underestimate the 'widow's mite'. It is one of the most powerful themes in human life. The Good Samaritan invokes a sense of admiration and regard in every breast. People need the opportunity to give as well as to receive. Confined for so long to the acceptable, charitable margins of life, it now needs to be placed at the centre of social relations.

The care and concern which giving and receiving require can only be given substance at a neighbourhood level, not a city-wide one. The security and comfort which comes from identity with and a feeling of belonging to a group can only be found in one of the many villages which make up the wider, more faceless city. It is only within each of these urban villages that a child, family and school can find the pride and spirit to both 'belong' and 'give' to friends as well as to 'receive' without becoming either grasping, dependent or aimless.

Existing methods of cognitive schooling and training have told modern planners (of architecture, roads, education or any facet of life) that they can rest the justification for their plans on their own professional judgement. They need not consult with 'lay' or ordinary people who are not 'experts', work with their hands – but not their brain – and, therefore, do not know what is best for themselves. Thus planners can design a building or road, or visualize an estate, a high-rise block of flats or a school secure in the knowledge that they are correct, that the citizen is wrong and has no right to question or shake the edifice of their superior opinion.

Yet these plans, which are prepared for and imposed on people, come unstuck in practice. They result in tower blocks which no one wants to live in, roads which lead nowhere and an education system which quite unintentionally teaches only failure and despair to the majority, the 80 per cent. This way lie the devastation of the 'carbuncles' and 'silos' at which Prince Charles tilts his lance and a divided, demoralized, uneconomical society as well as a deep popular suspicion of existing political parties and government.

Such plans waste the time and talent of professionals and squander large sums of public money. Worse still, they further destroy the confidence and erode the sense of belonging of the citizen. They reinforce the unintended message of the higher education system: that most are unable to shape their lives, chances and environment. The social division widens at the very moment when all cry out for it to narrow.

In the hands of those who do not care or who are politically motivated, this can cause social conflict. It is easily done. The apathy and resignation of 'why bother, they'll never listen' can quickly be provoked into the anger of 'they don't give a damn. They're alright, don't respect them, pull them down'. This way can lead to destruction; witness the events in Toxteth, Brixton, Handsworth and Moss-side.

To try to build from the 'bottom up' alone is as impractical and wasteful as imposition from the 'top down'. People know what they want for their communities, but alone they do not have the time, skill, information or confidence to build it. They need to employ others to help them see these tasks through. As with the teacher and the SG school, they need the catalytic effect of planners who are not working in isolation from the community, but with residents whose trust they have gained. The traditional planner's approach on its own can create the missile silos and concrete jungles of social despair. The 'bottom-up' approach on its own can lead to inner and outer city strife. Both approaches working together can form an equation, not just of planning success, but also of social cohesion. This equation not only applies to schools and other local institutions but it could also inject fresh life into a dangerously dated and weak political structure.

Plans which are requested by those who will have to live with the consequences and which are devised in partnership with trusted community-oriented planners do work. They are cost-effective and save time and energy because the subsequent product will become a respected and well-used feature of the community.

As a result, ordinary people gain confidence and pride in the knowledge that they played a part in building their own environment. Social barriers come down, divisions are healed and society benefits. It is an attractive prospect, but bringing the powerful levers of the community into alignment with those of the planner and politican is not easy. The new relationship implied between politican, planner and resident requires from each, an amended role and a new way of working.

Trained so as not to take the citizens' needs into account, the planner and politician must now learn to do so. Those who are unfamiliar with this style can feel threatened by it, for the planners and politicians are no longer the sole judges of the outcome and can be questioned, even employed, by non-expert residents. Full participation and accountability are new skills which planner and politician must acquire and practise with real people in real situations. They do not come overnight.

In turn, residents can no longer afford the luxury of resignation, indifference or anger. They cannot sit back and leave the planning and shaping of their community to

the State or expert and then offer idle, carping criticism from the sidelines. They must gain the confidence and will to help themselves by working closely with the planners and the parties.

Balsall Heath has beaten its own bounds. It has written its history (1992) and created its identity. It has declared itself to be an aspiring urban village. Druids Heath and Small Heath are gaining a similar pride through the ownership of their schools. How many such villages are there in Birmingham and other towns? How differently must the political parties and city departments organize their administrative arrangements in order to take these villages seriously into account? To be effective, city services must clearly focus upon particular groupings of eager individuals and local agencies which serve natural and willing communities. They cannot be imposed on a random, city-wide basis without in the end causing the whole city to decay.

Without undertaking the process of consulting people and enabling them to agree the boundaries of their areas, it is not possible to say how many villages there are in any particular city. In Birmingham there are at least forty-five, probably rather more. In other urban areas there may be more or less. Along with the individual and the family these urban village areas form the basic building blocks for community-oriented administration and planning. As there are nearly 450 schools in Birmingham this means that on average each urban village might contain ten schools. One of these schools may house the community education and enterprise centre which boasts a host of local support services.

Next to the family and the school, the street and the local village community are the most vital influence on the developing child and an essential support for the adult. They can provide an anchor which steadies the individual and helps him or her to withstand the rapid changes which buffet the soul in the wider technological and material world. Indeed, it could give people the strength to resist and tame these wilder features of the modern world. Every city will in future, therefore, need to place a great priority upon its ability to help many such communities to re-emerge from beneath the accumulated concrete urban jungle of yesteryear and exert their identities upon the physical and social geography of tomorrow. Today, the residents of the urban village need help to develop a common bond with each other and to identify their own well-being with that of their neighbours. How can the local authority's new children's and community departments envisaged in Chapter 11 help this process?

The following list of suggestions forms only a brief and introductory answer which might help to identify and name each village:

- Where are the boundaries of the village? Where are its entry and exit points? There is a point to making these obvious and distinctive, like postal district signs. How are residents and visitors to know when they are being welcomed within these boundaries or invited to return upon leaving?
- The character of a village is defined as much by its central, focal point as by entries and exits. It does not matter whether the centre is identified by shops, a library, a school or a community centre as long as it is clear to residents where the centre is. Does it have the right atmosphere, either because of its architecture or the quality of the services which it offers, or both?
- Perhaps a flag, crest or shield might help to give identity to both the entry gateways and the central features of the village.

- At Christmas, or carnival or some other community celebration both gateways and central features might be enhanced by festive decorations prepared by schools, churches and mosques and erected by the CEEC.
- The content and style of the celebrations will, of course, differ according to the particular community, but, whatever they are, they are important occasions, and the more people that take part in the planning and execution of them, the better. Such occasions emphasize the strengths of the community through sport or art, business or purely social events. They can highlight calendar festivals and the natural seasons which urban life might otherwise obscure.
- A building which functions as a village hall and meeting place and a village green or some kind of arena are important, not only to host celebrations, but to serve the needs of different interest groups which make up the community.
- Community notice boards which advertise events, and spread local news and information might help. A community newspaper would make the dissemination of information even more sophisticated and provide the village with its own voice while also helping to promote the schools of the village.
- Building and development plans which affect the life of the village often do not take strict enough account of its particular identity, or of the wishes of residents. It would be even more profitable and effective to build and develop in ways which highlight that identity, rather than to inhibit, depress, or even destroy it. The style and proportion of buildings, the materials used, the location of facilities, etc., are all crucial to the creation of harmony in a neighbourhood.
- This implies the need for effective consultation with and involvement by residents in local politics, suggesting some kind of non-party political community forum or council which is seen to represent the various aspects of the community.
- While the village will need the help and encouragement of an enabling city centre, its residents must be slowly weaned from too great a dependence upon it. They must become capable of generating a host of vital, autonomous, local activities.
- If it has no church or its residents hold different religious beliefs, then the whole village may at first find it difficult to uphold a set of basic moral values and codes of conduct. But communal life will not be complete without them. It is not necessary to take sides with one or other religious establishment to agree certain basic truths. These are best displayed as publicly and visibly as possible for the village community must develop and defend its own unique traditions and authority.
- While taking a growing pride in its own separate identity, each village will also need to make a contribution to the wider city and to benefit from those global tasks which can only be undertaken by a central organization. This contribution and dependence will be more fully appreciated because of the identity and sense of purpose which the village itself provides for its residents and their families. Just as the individual benefits from a strong family and communal life, so the urban village will benefit from a strong interchange between it and the wider town and society as neither can flourish on their own.
- Finally, the schools of each village will surely wish to 'lie athwart' the life of their catchment community and assist with its development. The CEEC which services and maintains the grounds and decorates the buildings of the village's schools can and should ensure that the whole village is neat, tidy, litter- and graffiti-free and signals that it is cared for and proud of itself.

It would make sense for the village school(s), the village green and hall to be the focal point around which an array of agencies would cluster, such as a health centre, advice centre and job creation office. Such a cluster of agencies would resemble a kind of mini-, local town hall. Nothing is ever perfect or complete. Different villages might come to assert one or other mix of the attributes outlined above although few will have the possibility of being purpose-designed and built, as is the case with Poundsbury. This village is to be constructed on farmland on the edge of the small town of Dorchester in Dorset. The idea was conceived by Prince Charles with the help of the celebrated architect, Leon Krier. The Prince, who owns the land, hopes that the new village will eventually comprise some 2,000 homes to house a population of 8,000 souls. A key feature of Poundsbury is that both terraced and detached houses, shops, offices and workshops will knit closely together so that a simple, ten-minute walk along its cobbled streets will enable the resident to reach any part of the village. At the heart of the first phase of building is to be a square which will be surrounded by shops and offices. The square will also contain a market hall. This will be raised on pillars to provide shelter and rest beneath it. The hall itself will house a café and meeting rooms. Alongside the hall a comforting, familiar, 25-metre-tall, square, church-like tower will be visible from all corners of the village. When the building is complete in a few years' time, the village will become the envy of many inner ring and outer city communities. With ingenuity and will, any urban area could be enabled to capture the atmosphere, calm and enterprise of village life.

THE URBAN VILLAGE, THE POLITICAL PARTIES AND THE ACTIVE CITIZEN

It would be a mistake to assume that the existing political parties and town hall government will be of direct use either to the urban village or to its schools without undergoing radical reform. The governors of independent schools will in effect take the place of the councillors who used to sit on the council committee which was part of the LEA. Indeed, representatives from the urban village may well cause some local councillors to disappear and those that remain to assume a different role.

Most residents, commercial, religious and other voluntary organizations in Balsall Heath, Druids Heath and a host of urban communities have felt over the years that their various efforts to build up the community have been ignored by the powers that be. Irrespective of which political party was in power in the town hall, the overwhelming feeling has always been that 'they' were remorselessly trying to knock the area and its institutions down even faster than local people could build them up. Local hopes, it seemed, too often came to nothing, while alien plans appeared as if from nowhere which rode roughshod over local feelings without any consultation. Somehow the relationship between the political parties, the planners and the local people has become so unproductive that many residents have come to question the democratic process and the possibility of serious participation within it. Just what is wrong and how can it be put right?

Democracy is supposed to be a system in which individuals are free to choose the kind of government they want, but, when the resident looks at the candidates standing for election, few recognize any politicians who have their interests at heart. At most

elections the resident is confronted by two or three candidates representing the big parties, and others who have little hope of election.

The trouble is that most councillors and Members of Parliament want to hold on to their positions of power, and have a deep, vested interest in maintaining the status quo. So, the core of each party is always re-elected and only the beginners and second-raters are placed in the unsafe wards and constituencies. If you live in a politically safe area you have no choice. If you are in an 'unsafe' area you can choose between learners and failures.

This is not all. In elections for Parliament the party machines turn out prepackaged policies which are designed to appeal to the party faithful, whose support is needed if a sufficiently large minority of the population is to be persuaded to vote the party into power. There is hardly any local content, and never anything definite enough for the resident to know whether or not they would like what the policy proposes. Even in local town hall elections there is very little that is local, and nothing at all that relates to particular urban villages because local political battles are used as tests of the popularity of the national Government and its nationwide policies.

Politicians, like professionals, tend not to live in the area they represent politically. They are allocated to a ward or constituency by a political bureaucracy and a few local activists, who themselves are far from being representative of the area. Typically, therefore, politicians commute to their constituency from other areas and are beholden to a political machine, a few activists and the policies of their party, rather than to the particular community they claim to represent.

Not only are the parties uninterested in those communities which are the secure fiefdoms of their opponents, they also do not try to become involved in the day-to-day life of the communities which they represent. As long as their electoral majority can be delivered in the few weeks run-up to an election they are content. Almost by conventional definition, politicians are concerned with gaining power in the town hall or Westminster, in order to implement their policies from the top down. They are not interested in or suited to wielding direct influence within the community at ground level or in helping it to build itself up. They are quite sure that they can best help their community or, rather, society in general by being re-elected and legislating change from above. Such legislation is clearly less to do with the needs of the community than with the theories and interests of the party to which they owe their seat and influence. These theories are not derived from serious or regular checking in the communities which the parties say they represent, but are self-selecting and more akin to faith than practical experience. Indeed, the theories of political parties which inform legislation are tested only amongst the dwindling numbers of party activists through the votes of safe constituencies, and the party's own supporters. Such theories are not falsifiable. They are not built from a process of interaction with real people in their struggle to develop their community.

Political parties, therefore, do not do justice to the many complex, day-to-day interests contained in each community, which are of real and continuing concern to residents and their families. Indeed, the parties tend to deny such interests. Great swathes of each urban village are, in effect, disenfranchised. The point can be illustrated as shown in Figure 12.1.

Only the activists within the circles A and B, within the wider community of C, are represented. The unwritten agenda of the community, D, is almost entirely omitted

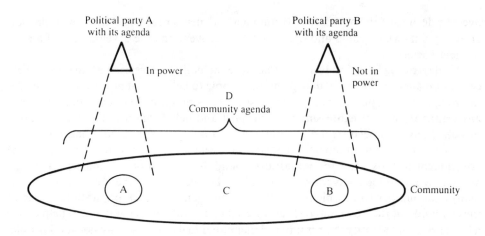

Figure 12.1 *Political parties and the community.*

from the policy of the party, partly because it remains largely unnoticed. Local people clearly understand that they are in effect excluded from the political process. This is perhaps why less than one third of the residents in most communities vote in a local election (which means that only half this number, 15 per cent, are represented by the party in power). They recognize that there is very little that they can do to influence the direction of policy. Their experience of the existing democratic process is that it is a kind of plausible confidence trick. It offers the illusion or form of choice and participation without their substance. Rather than try to develop or improve the situation – 'How can an individual buck the system?' – they shy away and ridicule both it and those activists and politicians who are left to try to make the process work.

Having lost the support of the people, it is little wonder that the weakened modern political party finds it difficult to exert its authority over the great bureaucracies of the State and local government which function as virtually autonomous empires. This is particularly true of local government where, of course, the councillors, unlike Members of Parliament, are unpaid, part-time volunteers.

It is difficult to see how a handful of volunteer local councillors can exercise any degree of serious control over huge town hall bureaucracies in order to make them serve the interests of particular villages. Serious democratic control only becomes possible when power is redistributed from both politicians and bureaucracy and placed in the hands of the various villages which make up each town. This redistribution of power is yet to happen in most aspects of city and urban village life, so we can begin to see why there is such a wide credibility gap between the people, on the one hand, and the planners and political parties on the other. This gap is not healthy for the parties or the planners. They become more and more detached from the people they claim to represent. It is not healthy for the people either as their views remain unrepresented and the energy and effort they expend between elections remains uptapped and unrecognized. It is not healthy for the political process or democracy, for they only thrive on a close, trusting relationship between people, party and Government. It is not healthy for the development of communities which need people and Government to be pulling in the same direction. It is little wonder that the politicians feel that they are presiding

over the decline of the once 'great' Britain and can neither see nor connect with the new growth points which could and should lead to recovery and the development of a new, resilient society.

This depressing situation has arisen because the political parties, with the subtle help of the bureaucrats, have persuaded enough people to believe that government exists for the good of the people and because the rest of the population do not feel that they have any legitimate way of expressing their disquiet and belief that it only serves the good of politicians who need strong government because it gives them jobs and power.

This is not to say for a moment that we can do without government. We need central government to look after foreign affairs, maintain law and order, and set a national agenda. We need local government to mediate between the competing demands of the many communities from which our cities are amalgamated, and to faithfully represent the city (and not their own interests and views) to central government and to help create a local pride and identity. Nor is it to say that individual politicians are not good people. Many are dedicated and sincere, working hard and long hours. Rather, it is the consequences of their collective actions which are of concern, for during the last hundred years, the political parties and the bureaucracies they nominally lead have increasingly demanded that government intrude into more and more areas of life. It now controls where people live, how they work, how they educate their children and how the sick and elderly are cared for.

There was a time when many of these things were not controlled and provided by central government. They were provided by people and organizations of their own free will. It was a time of more personal freedom. It is important to get back to that freedom and the social structures and institutions which give it real substance without going back to some of the material hardships of that time.

To regain that freedom means pushing the frontiers of government back so that it neither interferes with people's lives nor tries to regulate their initiative but enables them to live full lives. But if government is pushed back and refocused, then people must be prepared to do more for themselves and each other on an independent and voluntary basis. This is what is meant by a strong community; a community which does what it wants and looks after itself. It does not mean that people would be richer because of having to pay less taxes. People would still have to pay just as much in other ways for what they want, but they would get what they want. They would be more satisfied with what they got, and they should be more content with the way they are governed because they would have become a key part of that government.

Shortly before he was elected to the office of President of America, Bill Clinton said his government would 'steer more than it will row'. He was using concepts developed by David Osborne and Ted Gaebler (1992) in their exciting book, *Reinventing Government*. They make the point that modern governments have tried to both steer and row. That is, they have tried to steer the direction in which their nation or town is moving, they have set aims and goals for people and agencies to follow. At the same time, they have also tried to row by providing the means and agencies for achieving those goals. In attempting to perform both functions they have done neither very well. The country or town has seemed purposeless. The people and agencies have felt undervalued. Therefore, they have underachieved. Consequently services have been poor.

If it is to be effective, both central and local government must slough off the agencies and services which it has attempted to provide for people. These are better provided

through independent initiative. Such initiative can take the form of either private enterprise or public agencies which are funded by taxes, such as hospitals or schools. So, delegating the 'rowing' function to agencies which are independent of government does not entail 'privatization'. It merely means devolving the responsibility and finances for its provision.

Government may delegate the task of rowing, but it must still choose which services are required and raise taxes to pay for them. It cannot delegate the function of 'governance'. It is the special, irreducible task of government to set the style and shape of its country or region. Once freed from the task of rowing then a slimmer, high-minded government can concentrate on the job which only it can do, that of co-ordinating or steering the hopes, aspirations and priorities of its citizens.

Osborne and Gaebler say:

> Governments that focus on steering, actively shape their communities, states and nations. They make more policy decisions. Some even do more regulating. Rather than hiring more public employees, they make sure that other institutions are delivering services and so meeting their country's needs. In contrast, governments preoccupied with service delivery often abdicate this steering function.

They have become so busy with the impossible task of doing the rowing for everyone that they have failed to find the time to clarify where they are going.

Right-wing Conservatives who believe in the free-market would devolve both functions. They would 'privatize' the task of governance as well as that of service delivery. Such a nation would be rudderless. It would drift with the market and not be influenced by compassion or value.

The left, on the contrary, are so suspicious of the market that they would retain both functions. As a consequence, they would succeed only in creating bigger, not better, government. So, for different reasons, the extreme wings of each of the main parties both fail to identify the crucial steering and enabling role of government. They are, therefore, likely to view Osborne and Gaebler's opinions with suspicion and falsely accuse them, respectively, of either being too right- or too left-wing when in fact they are advocating a radical alternative middle way of organizing the tasks of government.

This helps us to understand why, in the past, left and right have spent so much time arguing with each other in what Peter Kellner described as 'irrelevant disputes about rowing, when the real clash of ideas should be about steering'. For decades, the choice seems to have been between raising taxes and greater public provision on the one hand or cutting taxes and reducing spending on the other, between more or less government; between government of the left or the right. This traditional choice has been misleading, even destructive. A third way forward exists.

Spending more does not make the outcome of that spending better. Increasing public taxes and the number of government projects can simply drain money down the black hole of bureaucracy. It can increase public dissatisfaction by hurting the pocket and producing mediocre services which compare unfavourably with the rigours of the private sector.

Equally, however, it is not easy to cut expenditure, for bureaucratic waste does not come in easily identifiable or

> neat packages. It is marbled through bureaucracies. It is embedded in the very way we do business. It is employees . . . working at half speed – or barely working at all. It is people

> working hard at tasks that are not worth doing, following regulations that should never
> have been written, filling out forms that should never have been printed

at each and every level of bureaucracy.

Waste in the corridors of government is substantial, but it cannot be reached by simply slashing at this or that budget. Right-wing governments can cut social programmes but they can thereby create more discord than existed in the first place. They may then be forced to buy their way out of their self-inflicted crisis. Osborne and Gaebler compare existing government with a fat person who must lose weight and who, therefore, needs to

> eat less and exercise more; instead, when money is tight they cut off fingers and toes. To
> melt the fat, we must change the basic incentives that drive our government.

The key question, then, is not about whether we need more or less government, but about the very nature of government itself. With Osborne and Gaebler (1992) we should be asking about what kind of government we need. Because the wrong question has been asked for so long, nations and regions have been ill-served. Vision has been lacking.

In defining the shape which his government would take, Bill Clinton said:

> I want a government . . . which is a catalyst for action by others . . . one that favours
> empowerment over just handing out benefits; one that believes in opportunity and respon-
> sibility more than entitlement.

Far from diminishing government, the single-minded concentration on the role of 'steering' is the best way of creating cost-effective, firm government. It mobilizes the energy and effort of people and agencies by setting them clear targets and aims, then trusts them to deliver the results more skilfully and energetically than any dependent government agency.

In other words, it is possible to see the previously distinct and politically opposed, destructive stances of collectivism and individualism as being capable of realignment. If redefined, shorn of the clutter of dogma, and located at their appropriate points in government and autonomous agencies and communities, they can be welded together into a powerful and productive new vision.

Osborne and Gaebler give copious working examples of how the new kind of government which they examine is already working at both central (federal) and local (state) levels as well as in many independent agencies and communities. Their overall vision merely identifies and orders what is increasingly happening and thus lends it weight and legitimacy. It can be broken down into ten interlocking components. These include:

- Government must steer and leave the rowing for others.
- Therefore, government must empower independent agencies and communities and not try to deliver services itself.
- In order to empower others, government must devolve authority and trust its citizens to respond to their new responsibilities. Devolution creates eager citizens, is democratic and highly cost-effective.
- It follows that government must break up its own and private monopolies and encourage competition between agencies.
- Competition means that independent agencies are forced to serve their customers and not their own institutional ends.

- Such customer-oriented agencies are not driven by rules but by missions, visions and values.
- The government can steer such agencies in its own democratically chosen direction by funding results or outputs rather than inputs which are costly and can lead nowhere.
- Both government and agencies can begin to focus on earning money and not just on spending it. It is possible to make many activities pay their own way. It is equally important to subsidize only those which cannot be underpinned by their own entrepreneurial efforts. The process is helped by giving customers who cannot pay credits or vouchers to buy services through shopping around in the market.
- Governments which try to steer and row tend to spend large sums of money on crisis management trying to cure ills after they have arisen. Governments which steer look into the future and spot crises before they arise. 'A stitch in time saves nine.'
- Finally, governments which steer solve problems and achieve results by 'leveraging the market place' rather than by simply creating public programmes. That is, government uses the entrepreneurial spirit to transform the public sector, invigorate and empower large private areas of society which have previously become dispirited through a dependence on poor, monopolistic public provision. This does not entail 'leaving things to the market'. Rather, it is a form of intervention within it. It uses the public purse in an entrepreneurial way to lever and influence the market. It combines public and private initiative rather than sees them as irreconcilable opposites. 'It is active government without bureaucratic government'. It places the old, pyramid-like bureaucracies of industrial society firmly in the past and looks forward to the different form and style of the new post-industrial society.

It is only now becoming clear just how radical and far-reaching is the change implied by the need to alter the role of the central authority and introduce to centre stage the role of enterprise and self-reliance in the community. Not only each citizen but also each political party must take this point very seriously.

From the passive to the active citizen

In the process of refocusing the range of functions and power of the town hall and the State two needs are exposed. One entails the local community in robustly helping itself through a range of socially oriented small businesses, community trusts, and other local institutions in addition to schools. The other concerns the means by which it can come to represent itself effectively without the aid of the political parties and the centralized bureaucracies which they previously tried to control. Both entail moving from a passive role for the citizen to an active, formative one which has substantial implications for the future role of political parties and the nature of their policies.

Parish councils have a legal existence. Rural villages which have retained these forms of local democracy elect their own parish councillors to represent their own very local concerns. They are able to levy a precept of one or two pence in the pound, which can give the parish councillors a useful income to dispense as they and their constituents see fit. They normally employ a parish clerk who services and acts for the parish just as St Paul's administrator helps local volunteers to organize their own bonfire night, carnival and village newspaper.

Many people would respond far more positively to their own urban village community or neighbourhood forum than to their party political councillor because they would see the immediate and positive results of their representations. Such bodies should be explicitly non-party political to ensure that they are able to take in all local views. They could be composed either of delegates from all local agencies, or, through voting for and electing members on a street-by-street basis, of elected representatives, or, like the new school governors, a blend of elected and co-opted representatives.

The conventional city officer and politician has to be loyal to office and party and cannot help the community to press the 'system' to help achieve its aims. In contrast, the parish or neighbourhood clerk, the community's own development officer, could be employed by the neighbourhood forum to reflect its interests and to act for its members, if necessary, against the judgment of city-employed peers and the political parties.

Like his or her community education (ICES) counterpart, the development officer's role might first be to give people confidence to formulate and express shared goals. Second, it could be to help them to press these goals upon the city authorities and to ensure that they are acted upon. The development officer's motto must be to 'aim high, then higher'.

In order to show local people that they can make the system work for themselves it is simultaneously necessary to work with city officers and politicians to convince them that helping local people to achieve their objectives is productive and cost-effective. In making the system work, it will be transformed. The rowing function which government once exercised will be diminished. The active citizen will fill the space which this aspect of government once occupied. A new partnership between people, planners and politicians is developing in which the steering politician must tell the planner to formulate plans in accord and consultation with the interests of local people rather than those of government, party or the planner.

The secret of the effectiveness of the transformed system lies in the fact that previously passive residents can, like school governors, become actively involved in both the upkeep and government of their own community. They can become responsible for its ills and advantages, in the place of remote authority. It is they who must remedy those ills and capitalize on those advantages. No one will do it as well as they will do it for themselves. At the same time, it becomes the task of the once intervening city centre officer and politician to respond, facilitate and enable the local agenda to be realized.

Although it is novel to the urban scene, the neighbourhood forum and its officer do not comprise an additional layer of government, which further complicates the organization of democracy. Rather, like the new school governors, they take the place of significant parts of the previously over-intrusive city councillor and planner who, as a consequence, can concentrate on their enabling, supporting and resourcing role.

Indeed, trusting local people with democracy may be so successful that each neighbourhood forum might put forward its own non-party political candidates to stand in local council elections to make sure that its wishes are respected. This could catch on and community candidates could come to represent their community in the town hall in place of party representatives. The process of local government would benefit enormously as it really would be local.

Because so many of the tasks once undertaken by the town hall can readily be discharged within each village it is necessary to reduce the size of the town hall. Just as in educational affairs power is swiftly moving from the politician and the planner to

the school and its community governor, so in most spheres of communal life decision-making should come to reside in the hands of local agencies and the local forum with the help of its independent community development officer. Therefore, almost all town hall departments can be slimmed down or even disappear in the way proposed for education. By the same logic, not only the number and nature of officers, but also the number and nature of councillors can be changed.

Old-style city departments were organized in terms of specialist professional functions – education, social services, housing, etc. – as well as in pyramid-like hierarchies. This was of little benefit to disintegrating communities which saw themselves as potentially integrated, thriving wholes. So, the new, community-oriented department will cut across the old boundaries and specialisms. Instead of being organized segmentally and hierarchically it will, like the maypole, subtend an array of mini-chief executives to the various neighbourhoods for which the local authority has elected responsibility. These neighbourhood executives could marshall and deploy the levers of local government to service and enhance the power of the communities' own growth points, through each village's own devolved town hall.

The role of the city councillor remains vital. It would be sensible, therefore, to increase the calibre and ability of those who do stay to control and direct the unelected, if shrinking, new-style professional bureaucracies. To achieve this task, far fewer councillors are needed. Their numbers can be reduced by at least half. Furthermore, it makes sense to pay the chairs of council committees in the same way that MPs are paid. It makes similar sense to elect and pay the mayor of each town. Strong candidates should stand for the office not as members of this or that party, but as clearly identified individuals. The post-holder should be paid and expected to play a vital role in the affairs of the local authority. Similarly, the chairs of departments should be paid and expected to behave in a non-party political manner.

A hundred years ago people asked parliament and local government to provide them with schools. Because these schools and other institutions of the welfare state were paid for by taxes, people also asked to be represented in parliament and the town hall via their political representatives. At the time, the struggle to win universal suffrage was as important as the right to win universal education. The two developments were interdependent.

Now that schools and other institutions are being passed from parliament and the town hall back to a more sophisticated and impatient people then it is also necessary to rethink the purposes and practices of the democratic political process. As a consequence, the political parties must reshape their agendas and develop with the times. They must undergo their own equivalent of the reforms which schools and local authorities are experiencing if people are to be provided with modern structures which help them to release their talents. If this important step is to take place a basic change must occur in the way the political parties think about society. This is the subject of Chapter 13.

REFERENCES

Hart, V. (1992) *Balsall Heath, a History*. Studley: Brewin Books.
Osborne, D. and Gaebler, T. (1992) *Reinventing Government*. Reading, MA: Addison-Wesley.

Collectivism and Individualism

All good things must come to an end. Over long periods of time individuals, agencies, even whole cultures and societies are, as it is said, grains of sand in the desert.

Karl Marx (1818–1883) was an intellectual giant. From the many signs of the times he developed a collectivist theory of history and social development. With the help of his theory he foretold how the emerging 'capitalist', industrial societies of the mid-nineteenth century would evolve and develop deep class divisions before revolution created a new 'proletarian' socialist or communist state. Society was, Marx thought, developing as a result of its own inexorable laws. This proved to be an attractive, compelling way of seeing the evolution of human society. It dominated the thoughts of many people for a century.

Marx was writing at the time of Charles Darwin (1809–82), who had just elucidated equally fresh and disturbing theories on biological evolution. Before Darwin, established thinkers and theories said that Man was the creation of God. Darwin placed man in the context of an earthly process of evolution and caused quite a fuss. Before Marx, people were convinced that people had free choice. Each individual answered to his or her conscience and God. Marx rubbished the concept just as severely as Darwin undermined the notion that Man had been created by God, who had given him the powers of thought and choice. Just as Darwin said that people evolved from and were part of the evolutionary biological process, Marx caused an even greater fuss by saying that society was also evolving and that modern man was the product of that social evolution. Choice and free will were deceptive illusions. Society makes man, man does not make society.

The age in which both Marx and Darwin were writing was that of the painful birth and growth of the modern town. It was also awash with scientific discovery and the realization that there were natural laws which, if harnessed, could bring great good and further help these towns to develop. Little wonder that Marx thought that he had uncovered 'laws' about society which governed how it behaved, which were akin both to the law of evolution which governed the biological world and the laws of science which governed the physical world.

Everyone now knows that Marx's political predictions which were based on his 'laws' proved to be glaringly false. These predictions could only be given temporary verity

through Lenin's and Stalin's brutal imposition of them in an attempt to prove them correct. They nonetheless held sway over millions of people for most of the twentieth century until countless little people proved them to be false by tearing down the Berlin Wall and the rest of the Iron Curtain. Yet it is important to distinguish between Marx's discredited predictions and the theory from which they were drawn, because too many people now think that in disposing of these predictions the whole of Marxist thought has also been dismissed. This is not true for, contrary to popular myth, the people of Eastern Europe have only rubbished Marx's predictions. The basic concepts on which his predictions were constructed, his view of man in society, are as alive in Britain and other Western societies as they were when Marx first fashioned them.

We must remember that Marx was merely one of the founding fathers of modern sociological thought. Others include Emil Durkheim, Max Weber and Sigmund Freud. Their distinct works were later synthesized by Talcott Parsons before entering into the culture, the atmosphere of modern sociological and popular thought.

Concepts like role, norm, social structure, rational legal authority and social system now come so readily to the practising and teaching sociologist that he or she no longer gives them a second or sceptical thought. With the spread and general acceptance of sociology, with its teaching in so many colleges and universities, a whole generation of sociologists, educationalists, other professionals and politicians have been taught in such a way that these deterministic, collectivist concepts are now uncritically accepted. They are taught as the very foundation of modern thinking about people and society.

The great German sociologist Max Weber helped to turn Marx's views about society into this sociological consensus by defining bureaucracy as the systematic application of rational legal authority. He deemed rational legal bureaucracy to be the greatest organizational force which history had witnessed. It laid to waste all previous traditional and religious forms of organization, enabled the development of Western industrial societies and helped them to conquer the world. Bureaucracy, he wrote (1968), 'revolutionizes with technical means . . . from without. It first changes the material and social orders and through them the people by changing the conditions of adaptation . . . It furthers the development of "rational matter-of-factness" and the personality type of the professional expert.'

Weber was disturbed by the implications of his analysis. He was concerned to think (1960) 'that the world would one day be filled with nothing but little cogs, little men clinging to little jobs and striving towards bigger ones . . . It is as if . . . we were deliberately becoming men who need order and nothing but order, who become nervous and cowardly if for one moment this order wavers and helpless if they are torn away from this total incorporation in it.'

The bureaucratic administration of human affairs which Weber wrote about at the beginning of the twentieth century was not only of value to the then-new science-based manufacturing industries, it was indispensable for the emergence of the welfare state. As Osborne and Gaebler wrote (1992): 'To keep the administration of the public services untainted by the influence of bribery and corruption a new breed of professional manager was created who could run the state bureaucracy in an efficient, business-like manner. Written exams, pay scales, protection from arbitrary hiring and firing, rules of conduct' became an essential part of the central and local civil service. They kept 'the politicians and bureaucrats from doing anything that might endanger the public interest' as defined by those at the top of the pyramid.

For most of the twentieth century this view of the way industrial society was organized and the collective caring policies which flowed logically from it prevailed. Again, as Osborne and Gaebler suggest (1992): the rationally administered state 'provided security – from unemployment, during old age. It provided stability . . . a basic sense of fairness and equality . . . It provided jobs. And it delivered the basic, no-frills, one-size-fits-all services people needed and expected: roads, highways, sewers' (and hospitals, schools, welfare benefits and nationalized industries).

However, this view could work only as long as the politicians and administrators who ran the pyramid-like bureaucracies had enough information to take reasonable decisions which those at the bottom of the pyramid 'could not query or improve upon; as long as most people worked with their hands and not their brains; as long as there were mass, indiscriminating markets; as long as most people had similar needs; as long as' the Western industrial nations had no serious competitors such as Japan which could rival them.

Today, this kind of world is fading into the past. In the high-tech, post-industrial society of which Japan is a model, 'people get access to information almost as fast as their leaders do. We live in a knowledge-based economy, in which educated workers bridle at commands and demand autonomy. We live in an age . . . in which customers have become accustomed to high quality and extensive choice.' Today it is no more acceptable for Henry Ford to say to his customers: 'You can have a model T car in any colour you want provided it is black' than it is to say: 'You can have any school you want provided it is the off-the-peg state school to which your child will be sent.'

As we learned from Valerie Stewart, Charles Handy and John Harvey-Jones, Ford, ICI and other large corporations were the first to change because of the competitive nature of Western societies' economic markets. The monopolistic nature of public services lagged behind. However, governments are now beginning to realize that unless they also change they will fail their customers, the voters, who will seek alternatives or simply become disaffected if such alternatives cannot be found.

In this new 'environment of post-industrial society the bureaucratic institutions developed during the industrial era – public and private – increasingly fail us. Today's environment demands institutions that deliver high-quality goods and services . . . . It demands institutions that are responsive to their customers, offering choices of non-standardized services; that lead by persuasion and incentives rather than commands; that give their employees a sense of meaning and control, even ownership. It demands institutions that empower citizens rather than simply serving them.' Indeed, it demands a very different kind of society to the one which Marx and Weber felt was inevitable and which their theories made universal. The new, post-industrial society clearly needs a different kind of theory to explain it, from which a quite different set of policy implications will flow.

The sociological and political consensus which Marx and Weber built has been slow to change. While it was constructed in and relevant to the industrial societies of the past it still patterns the thoughts and frames the judgments and policies not just of sociologists in their ivory towers but of most 'educated' people in positions of political influence. The more such people persist in using the old consensus to explain modern society and its needs, the more both the theory and its exponents become a constraint upon that society. An alternative theory is needed which locates its starting point in the arena of individual choice and free will which Marx rejected so decisively 150 years ago.

So, this alternative theory is not new. However, it may need to be adjusted and brought up to date if it is to be adequate to the task of understanding the modern world.

FROM COLLECTIVISM VERSUS INDIVIDUALISM TO THE INDIVIDUAL IN THE COMMUNITY

As the individual develops, so he or she gains a degree of distance and a qualified independence from those around him or her. In small, but significant ways, the situations through which he or she acts and gains knowledge differ from those which form the experience of others. Each person is, in certain respects, and to a greater or lesser extent both unique and a creature of the times and culture in which he or she is born. A blend of tradition and uniqueness expresses itself in each person's way of understanding self, the world and his or her desires.

Man's understanding of himself, his self-awareness, begins to form very early in life. From that point he himself enters as a vital determining factor in his own actions and beliefs and, in a complex way, into the future formation of his own personality. As such, he not only becomes resistant to whole ranges of possible types of social and psychological pressures, but actually participates in the formation and the alteration (whether intended or not) of those pressures. In other words, man becomes resistant to social or collective manipulation. Even the most compliant personality we can think of is resistant to such social 'pressures'. This is especially true if those 'pressures' tend to force individuals to rely on their own resources, or to change in certain ways which they recognize and which no longer accord with their ways of defining the world. They may seek to oppose such 'trends' by searching for others who wish only for the security of their own mutual identity.

This standpoint leads us to see social action as dynamic, changing, constantly forming and reforming. Whilst it suggests that social patterns (or structures) do form, they are recognized as made, imposed, sustained and changed by people. Man makes society. Society does not make man. If social life is a process of interaction between individuals and their environment, then any alternative view of social relations must include people and their stated wishes as a central feature around which the context of community turns. Things cannot be done for individuals, but only with them. People cannot be treated as objects, but only as subjects, as the key feature in any attempt to explain action or plan social developments.

The implications for government of this way of seeing individuals are obvious. In place of ordering, planning and legislating for people, whether in economic, social, educational or other spheres of life, it now becomes important to remove as many constraints as possible so that people can more effectively choose, construct and control their own way of life according to their ideals and will.

The freedom to choose will, in part, depend on the strength of the family and the social and cultural tradition from which an individual emerged and upon the degree of success which the enlightened State has in enabling the different choices of different people to be realized. An accurate, modern portrait of people-in-society acknowledges that the family and wider environment act not as the chains which bind people but as the springboard from which individualism can leap.

THE FAMILY

The family group and community from which each person builds their individuality is necessarily non-rational and traditional. A secure background and tradition is the ground upon which the individual can stand firmly and make a unique contribution to life. While the structures of collectivism diminish the family and other traditional communal institutions by doing things for people, thus elevating the role and functions of the state, individualism strengthens the family, supports traditions and builds local agencies so that people and community can be self-reliant, confident and strong.

We must think hard and long about how to help the family gain a more favoured and secure place at the very centre of social existence. How can parents be supported and helped to stay together? How can the pressures of work and materialism be countered to enable parents to spend more time with their children? How can parenting skills be most effectively taught to young people so that when they become parents they are more able to carry out the responsibilities of parenthood and withstand the temptations of a world without values? Unless we can answer these questions positively and with tangible, practical success, the growing individual will not gain the character and cultural framework which are the necessary springboards for the exercise of choice and creativity.

The collectivist State's care for the family is mediated through a variety of welfare benefits. The culture of this care not only suggests that there is no stigma or difficulty attached to being a single-parent family but regards anyone who questions this approach as uncaring and politically reactionary. Jack Kemp who was the Secretary for Housing and Urban Development in America has turned this approach on its head. He wrote (1992):

> Today our Welfare System provides millions of Americans with just enough cash to keep their heads above water. But it prevents them from saving, stops them from owning their own homes . . . and acquiring assets, discourages work, and most of all . . . subsidizes family break up. The combination of tax disincentives and a flawed welfare system has shattered the link between human effort and reward.

Peter Millar makes the point starkly in arguing that the welfare state has made it too easy for young, unmarried girls to have children and has provided:

> their children's fathers with an excuse for not marrying them. The result is an entire generation of teenage males who have grown up with no father figure and no expectation that they should ever shoulder social burdens in a world devoid of responsible, adult, male role models.

Wayne Bryant is a radical American democrat. He believes that disadvantaged people have been hindered, not helped, by welfare programmes. The poverty trap is perpetuated, not alleviated, by welfare care. He insists that 'the fact for poor people – not that they love the system – is that part of the present system is for them like a drug. Getting a cheque is like getting a fix. We need to get them off it.' The American experience shows that no matter how much money is spent, programmes of support are not a substitute for competent parents. So, new ways of assisting single-parent families are required. Further, fresh ways of bolstering the two-parent family are needed. These solutions are likely to entail major changes in the way the welfare state operates.

If we are serious about helping the young child to develop into a caring, mature, adult then a variety of means must be adopted which make child rearing more important and which extend a parent's responsibilities well into and beyond the child's teenage years. Etzioni's new book, *The Spirit of Community*, makes the point particularly well.

The strong collective state needs to be balanced and subdued by strong communities. Similarly, naked individualism needs to be tempered by caring and self-reliant community agencies. When they are remodelled, collectivism and individualism are not opposed to each other. They are natural complements which do not make sense without each other. Each contributes a vital ingredient to a full understanding of man in society. This holds true in all aspects of life.

SCHOOLS

The collectivist way of organizing state schools placed control and finance in the hands of large LEA bureaucracies. These bureaucracies managed schools on behalf of a compliant teaching workforce which had no experience of any alternative. Parents, the customers, were not even included in the equation. The result was an underutilized and under-resourced workforce at the chalk-face, customers who had no influence over either supply or product, schools which looked as if no one cared for or bothered to maintain them and standards which were too low.

Furthermore, this 'system' perpetuated an unequal division in which only a privileged 20 per cent gained a good education. This led them into positions of managerial influence over the other 80 per cent of the population, whose experiences of failure destined them for the factory floor and to be recipients of the services of the welfare state. While this 'system' suited the needs of industrial society, it could not service the needs of post-industrial society. Radical change was inevitable.

We are still in the early days of the resultant LM and SG reforms. However, ownership and control are passing into the hands of teachers, parents and community figures. The motivation which this gives school managers and parents is already leading to the prospect of rising standards. Schools are becoming more responsive to and a part of their neighbourhood. They are contributing to the development of a strong community and are beginning to change the 20:80 split into a situation where all pupils can anticipate educational success and the attribute of self-reliance.

HOUSING

Like LM and SG schools, the government legislation which enabled local council houses to be bought by their tenants was at first opposed by most councils, who wanted to go on building, controlling and managing them. The move proved to be so popular, however, that most people have changed their minds. Today, it is easy to spot those houses which are now privately owned: they and their gardens and fences are cared for; improvements have been made; they stand out in rows of otherwise uniform terraces.

At the same time as enabling individual families to own their own houses, the government also reduced council house building to a minimum. It increased the amount of

money available to housing associations to build houses in place of councils and forced the sale of empty plots of council-owned land to both associations and private house builders. This has not only enabled the utilization of otherwise derelict land, it has also replaced one monopoly supplier with a host of independent ones.

Some housing associations have become so large that they themselves risk becoming overbureaucratic and insensitive to local neighbourhood needs. But many serve only a limited geographical area and have developed a range of tenant services and a management style which fosters good neighbourliness and a sense of belonging. Many housing associations welcome their tenants to the neighbourhoods in which their houses are located. They provide them with information and advice about local services. They involve them in the process of management and the provision of security. They brighten the environment and streets with hanging baskets and iron-work through projects which also provide training and jobs. Some would argue that the development of the housing cooperative movement is of even greater value to local people in developing a shared sense of ownership and involvement. By the same logic, the idea of the Housing Action Trust, which takes responsibility from the city for an entire estate and hands it to the tenants, is a radical and imaginative step.

The net outcome is that in place of one uniform, drab, remotely managed set of state-provided and state-managed houses there has arisen a combination of privately owned houses and a range of locally managed ones which foster a sense of belonging and which are managed by boards of local, voluntary directors. In turn, of course, this has persuaded most city housing departments and committees to become much more imaginative in the way they manage their own remaining houses.

THE ENVIRONMENT

Prince Charles (1989) became

> increasingly aware of the failure of the current planning rules and regulations to create a supportive environment. It is not that there is any shortage of red tape; after all, every building that has been put up since 1947 has had planning permission, except for those associated with agriculture and Government activities. It's hard to believe sometimes, but the whole contemporary, built world has been through the mill of bureaucracy, committees' negotiations and often long and expensive public enquiries. To what end?

He said that he had

> canvassed the views and advice of all sorts of people with a profound interest in the subject, and the result has been distilled into a new set of suggested ground rules. By standing back and looking at what has been happening as objectively as possible, I could see that we seem to have forgotten some of the basic principles that have governed architecture since the Greeks. Many of them are simple common sense, like the laws of grammar that create a language.

He suggested

> that if in the name of progress you destroy the past, or consistently deny its relevance to the present, man eventually loses his soul and his roots. In order to avoid repeating the obvious mistakes of the last forty or fifty years it is essential to appreciate that certain values and principles are eternal ones, in terms of human experience. Because our tech-

nology changes so rapidly it does not mean our spirits, or our fundamental psychological responses, alter as well. Being modern and up-to-date does not mean we have to invent a new style or some new, revolutionary building material every other year.

Prince Charles went on to outline his principles of good practice which any building should conform to. There are ten of them. They can be summarized as follows:

1 *Land*.

We must respect the land. It is our birthright and almost every inch of it is densely layered with our island's history.

2 *Hierarchy*.

When we build upon the land the scale of our constructions should reflect their importance and their design should be comfortable and comprehensible to the users.

3 *Scale*.

Buildings must relate first of all to human proportions and then respect the scale of the buildings around them.

4 *Harmony*.

Each building that goes beside another has to be in tune with its neighbours.

5 *Enclosure*.

The scale can be large or small, the materials ancient or modern, but cohesion, continuity and enclosure produce a kind of magic, security and identity.

6 *Materials*.

Our rich variety of building material is a source of constant pleasure and surprise . . . Each town and village (should have) a different hue, a different feel and foster a fierce loyalty in those who belong there.

7 *Decoration*.

Living in a factory made world is not enough. Beauty is made by the unique partnership of hand, brain and eye.

8 *Art*.

While decoration is concerned with repetition and pattern, a work of art is unique. Why is it that contemporary artists play such a small part in the creation of our surroundings?

9 *Signs and lights*.

Far too many of the marks of twentieth century progress take the form of ugly advertising and inappropriate street lighting, apparently designed only for the motor car.

10 *Community.*

> People should be involved willingly from the beginning in the improvement of their own
> surroundings . . . The right sort of surroundings can create a good community spirit . . .
> People are not here to be planned for; they are to be worked with. In the creation of new
> communities the problems may be more difficult; but there is always local knowledge and
> that is where community starts.

Prince Charles believes that 'when a man loses contact with the past he loses his soul'
(p. 10). He talks of the need for proportion and harmony in life which can only come
from the way we construct and rebuild our modern communities. He insists in a rapidly
changing world:

> with new technological breakthroughs every other day, what on earth is wrong with people
> desiring surroundings which are familiar, traditional, well-tried and beautiful? Such a
> desire doesn't mean that we are any the less 'modern'; that we are suddenly going to revert
> to a pre-industrial existence and behave in an eighteenth-century fashion. Far from it. It
> seems to me that such a union of apparent opposites is essential for our sanity in today's
> world. What is so badly needed is for the architects, and the developers who employ them,
> to be more sensitive to the deep-rooted feelings of 'ordinary' people and to find ways
> of integrating their opinions and their need into the creative processes from which new
> buildings emerge.

Such a framework of principles and values as the Prince outlines could, he feels,
be used to great effect 'in rebuilding the shattered remnants of our inner cities so that
people once again have proper communities in which to live and which, in turn, restore
life and soul' (p. 14).

This is surely why the Government's policy to sell council houses to their tenants has
been such a success and why it makes sense to involve tenants in the management and
maintenance of whole estates. Of course, the building of council houses was as well
intentioned as the allocation of welfare to single-parent families. In both cases, however, the unintended consequences have caused basic human attributes to atrophy and
the quality of life to diminish. What many years ago was intended as the radical new
and caring initiative has come to haunt modern society as the conservative and soulless.

ECONOMICS AND THE ORGANIZATION OF SOCIETY

While the family, house, school and a well-designed community and town can provide
the individual with an excellent start in life, the way the wider town and society are
organized can help or hinder his or her development. Eric Schumacher (1974) wrote that
Small Is Beautiful. He proclaimed this, not just because it confined organizations to a
human scale but also because it makes good economic sense.

He wrote:

> Economic calculus, as applied by present-day economics, forces the industrialist to elim-
> inate the human factor because machines do not make mistakes which people do. Hence
> the enormous effort at automation and the drive for ever-larger units. This means that
> those who have nothing to sell but their labour remain in the weakest possible bargaining
> position. The conventional wisdom of what is now taught as economics by-passes the poor,
> the very people for whom development is really needed. The economics of giantism and
> automation is a left-over of the nineteenth-century conditions and nineteenth-century

thinking and it is totally incapable of solving any of the real problems of today. An entirely new system of thought is needed, a system based on attention to people, and not primarily attention to goods – (the goods will look after themselves!). It could be summed up in the phrase, 'production by the masses, rather than mass production'. What was impossible, however, in the nineteenth century, is possible now. And what was in fact – if not necessarily at least understandably – neglected in the nineteenth century is unbelievably urgent now. That is, the conscious utilisation of our enormous technological and scientific potential for the fight against misery and human degradation – a fight in intimate contact with actual people, with individuals, families, small groups, rather than states and other anonymous abstractions. And this presupposes a political and organisational structure that can provide this intimacy . . .

The collective state provides people with work and goods which make them dependent. When people are expected to take part in making the goods they need they become self-reliant and independent.

MODERN BUSINESS ORGANIZATIONS

Many private and nationalized industries became too large either to be efficient or to hold the loyalty of their staff. Schumacher's point applies with equal force to both types of industry, for his is not a political point but a practical one about the inefficiency of the large-scale organization and the effectiveness of the small unit. Valerie Stewart (1990) and Charles Handy (1989) provided contrasting models of how long-standing businesses could become so top-heavy that they could no longer deliver the goods and faced going out of business, or they could adopt a different way of organizing their affairs, reform and thrive.

We first illustrated the point in relation to LEAs, but it applies to all kinds of organizations. Those which are successful are characterized by 'decentralisation, bureaucracy-busting, shortened lines of authority, greater encouragement of innovation and risk-taking'.

Of course, the private company which did not adapt went out of business and was replaced by lean, efficient rivals. However, the State's own monopolies such as coal, steel, health and education initially faced no serious opposition. In each case change and development could only begin if central government legislated for change and divested itself of its own monopolies. Whilst the bureaucrats and the trade unions were furious, the customer began to benefit. The sleek, modern organization pioneered in post-Imperial Japan is now rightly beginning to hold sway in Europe and this country. Flatter, more individual, it functions in smaller units than was thought possible in previous decades.

CHARITY

To St Paul, charity was the basic building block from which the human relations of the family and community were constructed. It suffused and breathed life into hearth and home, church and neighbourhood. Because people could easily both give to others and receive through these institutions, their lives were enriched and made purposeful. Community was strong and resilient.

In modern times the power which the welfare state wields over most people's lives is extensive. The stabilizing effects of the family, community and religion were sacrificed on the altar of large-scale organization and material progress. Consequently, it has become easier for the young, innocent and vulnerable to follow the latest whim of fashion and to give vent to their passions irrespective of the judgements of tradition and value.

For most of its existence in Balsall Heath, St Paul's educational charity felt isolated and powerless as it struggled against the tide of events to demonstrate that if local people took control of their lives, and built and ran their own institutions, then standards and spirit would rise and the quality of life would be enhanced. Now it is being joined by a host of new independent state schools with thousands of new school governors and there is a real prospect of whole neighbourhoods beginning the difficult task of reconstructing their communities. It is within these communities and the urban village that the giving and receiving of charity will again thrive. This will endow urban life with meaning and value.

VALUES AND MORALITY

While discussing the pyramid and maypole in relation to LEAs we noted that the pyramid provided its own producer-oriented reason for existence which bent others to its will: what's good for the organization is good for the community. The maypole necessarily serves ends beyond itself: what's good for the community is necessarily good for the organization. As with charity, values and morality are ignored as illusions by collectivist theories. Yet they are defining features of the human condition which both explain action and give it point.

The kind of secular, amoral education and society which rational bureaucratic organization demands is quite different from that envisaged and created by the great traditional values, cultures and religions of earlier times. When the Home Secretary visited the central mosque in Balsall Heath, Dr Nazim, the chairman of the Mosque's Trust told him that, 'Education is an obligation to our children for which we are responsible to God.'

Dr Nazim went on to explain that this moral responsibility to God was part of a whole way of life which gave it a central and secure meaning. It did not just relate religion or culture to education, but to the raising of children to become caring, responsible adults and also to the family, work and leisure. The Muslim community in Balsall Heath live by this traditional value and are proud of it. Without it they fear that life would be meaningless and beyond their control. As Dr Nazim said, 'Control of destiny is lost if morality is shirked.'

This traditional, non-rational, but internally consistent and logical approach to life has been brought to Balsall Heath and Birmingham by Muslims from the East at exactly the time when the effect of the host society's bureaucratic rationality is causing Christian congregations to dwindle and churches to close. No wonder the world of Islam fears the world of the West and will presently open its own brand of self-governing state school, to make sure that its children are taught within the context of their faith. Once, like Islam, the Christian church informed all aspects of life. Today, Christianity is confined at best to Sunday, at worst to history. It has little formal or practical relevance today. Despite its compelling document, *Faith in the City* (1985), the Church of England feels

it has no battalions to combat the bureaucracy which has laid that city to waste. No alternative, modern culture or value has yet arisen in its place. Certainly today's code of amoral rationality offers no alternative to the soul, no spirit for the community, no guide or standard for the child. The value of reason which is sufficient for the State bureaucracy and officer has proved incapable of providing a substitute for home and hearth. The streets are bare and litter strewn, broken by patches of decay, bulldozed houses, bricks and rubbish. The crime rate soars. A sense of hopelessness hangs like a fog in the atmosphere.

The morality of the East has something to show the West. It can remind the host society of the codes by which it once lived. It can help to rekindle a spirit, a soul, a will in otherwise spiritless and unconfident communities. The newcomer can trigger the antidote to a major illness within the host society from which it alone cannot recover.

Neither native Caucasian nor Afro-Caribbean inhabitants of inner and outer areas are likely to undergo a sudden conversion to the values of Islam, although an interesting number do so. But the very presence there of the Islamic, Hindu and Sikh religions and their traditional cultural values of family life and neighbourliness is today an invaluable cement holding those areas together and keeping complete disintegration at bay.

Imagine that no newcomers from the East had come to Balsall Heath to take the place of those residents who had moved to the outer areas. It is difficult to believe that the community would now exist. The task of St Paul's would have been impossible. In addition to a social cement, these religions provide an example, a salutary lesson. Their sense of profound shock at how brazenly careless and immoral the host society is should cause us to ask just how far and pervasive the effect of the rationalization of life has become. If this is not sufficient, then the press and TV images of Bristol, Liverpool or Handsworth burning should clinch the argument.

Humans are by definition spiritual, moral beings. Create an environment which denies this fact of social life and a recipe for disaster and/or revolt results. To counter this remorseless modern trend, any politician or teacher has an obligation, if not to God, then to the child and community to help build the circumstances which celebrate and uphold the individual's need for spiritual love and clear standards by which to live.

A NEW THEORY

It is possible to illustrate the implications for a theory of society of the family, school, housing, environment, economy, business, charity and values by recalling the earlier triangular diagrams (Figure 8.1) which pictured the LEA and individual schools. This time (Figure 13.1), the main triangle stands for the State and society, not just the town hall and LEAs. The little dots stand not for schools but for people and the small triangles represent not just self-governing schools but all local agencies and institutions.

The collectivism of Figure 13.1a (the sociological and socialist consensus) and the unrestrained individualism of Figure 13.1c (right-wing conservatism) are polar extremes. The maypole-like Figure 13.1b (the radical alternative) represents a blend of the two extremes which corresponds both to the way successful modern businesses are organized and to the new independent state schools and communities. It highlights both the role of the individual and local agency and the social context in which that individualism is expressed. It suggests a partnership rather than polar opposites, harmony rather than conflict. Except for those who do not believe in 'society', the

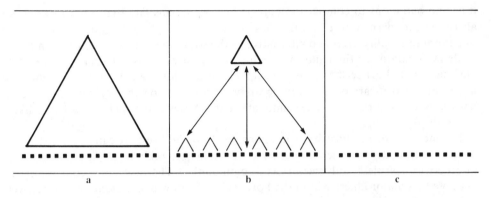

Figure 13.1   *The nature of organization implied by collective and individual theories when opposed and combined. (a) The pyramid collective organization. People bound together by the rules and institutions of the State. (b) The maypole blend of individualism and collectivism. People bound together by local communities and values. (c) Total individualism – anarchy.*

unadulterated individualism of Figure 13.1c is self-evidently not applicable even to many economic aspects of human affairs or it risks doing the same sort of damage to reality as the imposition of Marx's collectivist theories have done. So, it is sensible to compare and contrast the pyramid-like collectivism in Figure 13.1a, which Marx, sociologists and the industrial world successfully imposed on the human world, with Figure 13.1b, the maypole, which seems to bear the closest resemblance to the emerging reality of social relations in post-industrial society. A number of telling points can be made, which are listed in Table 13.1.

Perhaps it should be stressed that pyramid-like organizations make it difficult for the environment, charity, value, the urban village and the character of man to thrive. Maypole-like ones stimulate them by refocusing government and creating an enabling state. The enduring, traditional qualities of life are heightened by the radical alternative of the maypole. These include wisdom, humour, spirit, will and vision. The theoreticians of collectivism hardly recognize these characteristics. They are omitted from their analysis, explanations of and policies for society. The radical alternative gives them pride of place. They are irreducible entities – the catalytic spark of life without which neither explanation nor policy can be complete.

Whole societies and organizations within them do not just fit one or other typical pyramid- or maypole-like model. As Handy and Stewart point out, maypole-like organizations can easily become routinized and come to resemble pyramid-like ones, as has happened to the once-radical institutions of industrial society. These can survive for a while, but they will either disintegrate or go through a process of reform until they come to resemble the maypole.

Britain, other Western societies and organizations within them are at the moment in the painful process of transition from being pyramid-like to becoming maypole-like. While some within these societies still look to the past through collectivist eyes, others increasingly seek to accelerate the dawning of a new, post-industrial era.

Table 13.1 *A comparison of the values of collectivism versus a combination of individualism and collectivism.*

Collectivism	Blend of individualism and collectivism
Tradition, the family and local institutions are diminished	Tradition, the family and local institutions are upheld
The organizations' systems of rules dominates the individual	The individual is able to stay in control of events
Initiative is stifled	The individual is stretched
Innovation is rare	Innovation is the rule
Development is feared	Development is encouraged
There is a rigid hierarchy of authority and no scope for change. The lower ranks can only challenge this authority by rebelling or leaving the system	There is a natural hierarchy of talents and functions with plenty of scope for change. The individual and collective are reconciled through participation
Rigidity encourages disrespect, especially from the lower ranks whose talents are unrecognized. This leads to conflict	Flexibility encourages respect. There is a natural harmony or balance in social relations
There are no leaders. Individuality and variety are discouraged. It is the rules of office not the individual which are respected	Charismatic leaders are at a premium. Individuality and variety are encouraged. The office rules can be bent and re-created to get things done
The individual feels lost and isolated within a machine-like system	The individual identifies with the community and organization and gains fulfilment through them
People are dependent. The 'system' binds people together	People are self-reliant. Values bind people together

It is possible to conclude that, in an impossibly idealistic and theoretically misguided collectivist attempt to create from the injustices of industrial society an equal one, the political parties built an over-indulgent welfare state. This has diminished man's individuality, his need to take responsibility for himself and others. This resulted in poor service to the community and a democratic process which shone only in comparison with the communist block. The individual, character, local effort and charity became derided concepts, equated only with society's rejects or with the provision of individually tailored services for a wealthy and powerful few, who possessed the means and ambition to manipulate the otherwise constraining system for their own ends or who had the imagination to create for themselves private agencies which blossomed free from collective and political restraint.

The attitudes of politicians of both left and right became increasingly polarized. On the one hand, collectivist state institutions were defined by steering and rowing governments as being in the best interests of society. These institutions demanded and got attention and resources. On the other hand, individual or private institutions were regarded as being relics of a past, traditional age and were derided and starved of sustenance. They came to inherit the periphery of industrial society (see Figure 13.2) until the demands of post-industrial society required them to be reconsidered.

We can now understand that the long-standing polarization between public and private, collective and individual, State and community is not soundly based. It has

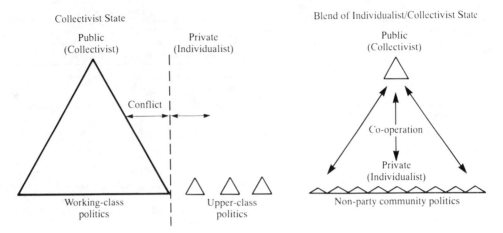

Figure 13.2   *The industrialist–collectivist and post-industrial models of society.*

disturbed the fundamental balance which man-in-society needs if life is to be healthy and productive.

This polarization has been harmful to the State, for it has made it cumbersome and unwieldy, inefficient and unattractive. It has robbed it of a natural authority, alienated people from it and caused it to use naked power to assert its position. Further, it has also placed artificial brakes upon social development and squandered individual initiative, effort and will. It has denied the spirit and soul of people, which rely for sustenance more on tradition and values than on reason. This prevailing way of seeing people in society is no longer relevant. It is in need of swift and radical reform. It is possible to discuss an alternative view which incorporates both the collective and the individual, the public and the private. It sees them as being in mutual alignment and as the driving force in social relations. The essential distinction between the two views is illustrated in Figure 13.2.

The development of a theory which combines the virtues of both collectivist and individualistic ways of organizing social affairs could mark the end of a period of major debate and conflict, between those who argued for a caring public state, and those who have advocated private initiative.

As post-industrial society emerges from the cocoon of constraint, we must accept that it has for too long been supposed that only the well-educated 20 per cent of the population, the confident, ambitious and affluent, are competent to run their own independent institutions, look after their own houses, use private health care and private schools and run their own businesses. Similarly, for too long it has been assumed that the poorly educated 80 per cent of the population were so incompetent and dependent that they could only be housed, made healthy and educated within institutions which the State provided and that they not only could do none of these things for themselves but also that to dream of doing so should be positively discouraged.

It is no longer necessary to use such dated suppositions and theories to form a policy which holds back the independent few in a vain, socially unbalancing attempt to make them equal to the dependent majority and to uphold this act as if it were a caring virtue. Rather, the time has come when the natural privileges of independence and autonomy,

which the ambitious were bold enough to forge for themselves, should be ungrudgingly offered to the many through the radical redefinition of the aims and functions of the State and the individual and the role of government.

Government needs to play a new, sleek, charismatic role which steers, stimulates and complements independent (public and private) initiative. Just as there needs to be a mixed economy of public support for private wealth generation, so there needs to be a similar mixture of public and private initiative in the fields of education, leisure, housing and community development. Once the public State has introduced the principle of independent community educational provision in its own state-financed schools then the age-old distinctions between public (i.e. state) and private (i.e. independent) schools will begin to dissolve. The result will be self-governing state schools and an array of thriving communities.

Unless more politicians, theoreticians and planners accept and understand this essential point they will neither be able to help people to construct the kind of communal, grass-roots institutions which the individual needs to become self-reliant, nor build the kind of enabling post-industrial State which is congruent with a mature society. So, it is important to consider how both the collectivist planner and politician and the unconfident individual can be helped to form a new partnership.

Sir Ralf Dahrendorf made the point well when he said that in future 'individuals will have to appreciate that philanthropy is a social obligation; companies will have to understand that it is their enlightened self-interest' to give and to be involved in the life of the community in which they are situated. Above all, said Sir Ralf, 'we need a pact between Government and the voluntary sector which preserves all the sensitivity and flexibility of private action, but involves a major share of government funding.' The urban school's use of its own budget and the entrepreneurial functions of the community education and enterprise centre illustrate that 'government funding' does not mean 'grant' aid or the 'redistribution' of wealth but the use of finance and the organization of society in quite different, new ways.

The devolution of responsibility for the delivery of most services from central and local government to communities is good news for the citizen as well as for quality and efficiency, but it is very bad news for those bureaucrats who are made redundant because their tasks are performed by people in the community and for those politicians whose power is diminished because the authority of the individual has been enlarged. For them, it means that the concepts and structures of parliamentary and democratic socialism, which have sustained them for a century, are now just about as irrelevant in this country as single-party communism is in Eastern Europe. Like the redundant factory worker, they need the support of redeployment schemes to help them to adjust to changed circumstances. Otherwise, like the East European communist, they will find ways of entering the new organizations and slowing the pace of change.

REFERENCES

Archbishop of Canterbury's Commission on Urban Priority Areas (1985) *Faith in the City*. London: Church House Publishing.
Atkinson, D. (1971) *Orthodox Consensus, Radical Alternative*. London: Heinemann.
Bendix, R. (1960) *Max Weber, An Intellectual Portrait*. London: Heinemann, p. 455.

Etzioni, A. (1993) *The Spirit of Community*. New York: Crown Publishers.

Gouldner, A. (1970) *The Coming Crisis of Western Sociology*. London: Heinemann.

Handy, C. (1989) *The Age of Unreason*. London: Hutchinson.

HRH The Prince of Wales (1989) *A Vision for Britain*. London: Doubleday.

Kemp, J. (1992) *Sunday Times*, 10 May.

Nisbet, R. (1966) *The Sociological Tradition*. London: Basic Books.

Osborne, D. and Gaebler, T. (1992) *Reinventing Government*. Reading, MA: Addison-Wesley, p. 74.

Schumacher, E. (1974) *Small Is Beautiful*. London: Abacus.

Stewart, V. (1990) *The David Solution*. Aldershot: Gower Publishing Company Limited.

Weber, M. (1968) *Economy and Society*, vol. 1. New York: Bedminster Press, p. 245.

Contents

To Sophie and Jane and their friends

Sayings

I QUESTION: Who first coined the saying 'A camel is a horse designed by a committee'?

ANSWER: I don't know, but I expect it was the same person who said 'An elephant is a mouse designed to Government specification'.

II The characteristic of our time, and the mark of a technological civilization is the disproportionate growth of administration in relation to quality and indeed as an end in itself . . . I'm afraid that this baneful development is very evident in public education. More and more control of our education tends to be administrative rather than cultural . . . The view I want to put to you is that administration is only safe when it is in the hands of the philosopher and thinker, the teacher and the artist . . . for whom administration exists merely as the instrument for realizing quality and value. Such people are always economical of their use of administration.
(Henry Morris, chief education officer, Cambridgeshire)

III Yet there is hope. Slowly, quietly, far from the public spotlight, new kinds of public institutions are emerging. They are lean, decentralized and innovative. They are flexible, adaptable, quick to learn new ways when conditions change. They use competition, customer choice, and other non-bureaucratic mechanisms to get things done as creatively as possible. And they are our future.
(David Osborne and Ted Gaebler)

Preface

The infant discipline of sociology came of age in the nineteenth century as rational, scientific man emerged from the tradition of religion and struggled to explain his place in the ferment of the Industrial Revolution. Perhaps understandably, the early sociologists laid such emphasis on the part which the novel concept of the 'structure of society' played in governing people's behaviour that they developed a determinist view of it: 'Society makes man, man does not make society.' Choice, free will, character and value were illusions, figments of the irrational thinking of an earlier age and powerless in the face of the 'process of socialization' and the iron forces of industrial society. In turn, this emergent sociological viewpoint helped to form and legitimize the enlightened thinking of those who built the welfare state: things must be done for people as they cannot help themselves.

In 1967 Professor Robert Nisbet wrote that the modern 'process of moulding the still ductile forms' of sociology from its nineteenth-century origins 'can't go on forever. Sooner or later the process of revolt, of abandonment of "chrysalids" of concept and method take place. Perhaps it is taking place in our own day before our unseeing eyes . . .' In 1971 Robert Nisbet was kind enough to say of my first book, *Orthodox Consensus, Radical Alternative* (Heinemann), that 'through the author's eyes we see, as no other book makes us see, the utter bankruptcy of conventional sociological theory . . . Atkinson's book makes us understand very well indeed why, as things now stand in conventional sociology, boys are made overnight into old men without ever passing through youthful maturity.' If sociology has become senile and ill-equipped to understand man in modern society, what implications does this have for the nature of the modern state?

Having argued my way out of the ivory tower and conventional sociology I found myself in Balsall Heath, one of Birmingham's inner areas. I have lived there or thereabouts ever since and accumulated a set of experiences which have confirmed in me the notion that sociology is indeed powerless to explain how ordinary people live, work and die. These experiences have also demonstrated that the modern welfare state, which sociology has striven to explain and which it has done so much to legitimize, is also built on dated and crumbling foundations. It fails to connect with much of the

human character and people's everyday aspirations. While sociologists still do their best to sanctify it as the zenith of human development, it is abundantly clear that ordinary people know rather better. They feel it limits their potential. They are constrained by it, not liberated.

So, the accumulated experience of the last twenty-two years has shown me that most people require a fresh way of explaining their lives and enhancing and building towards their hopes. Goody, Tom, Vino, Tess and Ada demonstrated to me that the need was urgent. Since their early tuition many residents of Balsall Heath have refined the lesson which they taught me.

This book discusses their fears and hopes. It offers an agenda for action which could quell the former and help to realize the latter. As such, the book has been written for two, equally significant, sets of readers. First, it is an essay in community education, for teachers, heads, governors, parents and educationalists. It is about how standards can be raised by making schools self-governing, proud, community agencies. Second, the book also shows how the fabric and standards of urban communities have broken down. It is written for all those interested in the revitalization of urban neighbourhoods and communities – residents, professionals of all kinds, city officers and politicians. It is about community development, using schools as a prime example of how various agencies can be returned to the control of local people.

The reader who is interested in schools and community education will wish to read the three parts of the book in sequence. The reader who is more interested in community development and the need to refocus government may wish to read Parts 1 (Chapters 1 to 6) and 3 (Chapters 11 to 15) before returning to Part 2 (Chapters 7 to 10), which looks in detail at the structure and content of the self-governing school.

The book could not have been written without the support and understanding of my wife, Gill Atkinson. It has gained much from the helpful textual work and suggestions of Diona Gregory. I am very grateful to her. I have also benefited from countless discussions with Dr Anita Halliday, Val Hart, Steve Ball, John Rennie, Professor Tim Brighouse, Sir Richard Knowles, Jim Amos, David Swinfen, Josh Hart, Ian Edwards, Anne Hynes, Jacqui Ure, Seeyam Brijmahun, Bryan Stoten, Joseph Quamar, Pat Preistman, Wally Rose and Ted Wright. In addition to their assistance I have had help from such a large number of teachers, parents and politicians that I can't name them all. Most of the good ideas are theirs. The mistakes are mine.

August 1993

The author has produced a detailed 'DIY Tool Kit' for schools which are considering becoming self-governing. It contains a range of materials designed to ease the transition. It also shows local authorities why they have nothing to fear from self-governing schools. Indeed, it explains how they can benefit.

Those interested in the Tool Kit should contact Dr Dick Atkinson, 19 Mayfield Road, Moseley, Birmingham B13 9HJ (telephone: 021–449–3803).

Chapter 1

Introduction

Many people are profoundly dissatisfied with the quality of life in inner city and outer urban areas and with the style and standards of urban schools in Britain. The very cores of the country's great towns and cities appear to be blighted with an array of intractable social, economic and educational ills. These plague the spirit and lower morale. The political parties appear only to manage the process of decline. They do not seem able to touch the fears or tap the aspirations of ordinary people or the growth points of society.

It is hard to recall that only a century or so ago the towns of Britain were being developed in an excited response to the scientific and manufacturing revolutions which drove the culture and politics of the times. It was in those days that the town halls of today were boldly constructed, while alongside them the first education authorities were organized. In turn, they built new schools with the aim of making literate and numerate the children of labourers who had come from the rural fields to work in the dark satanic mills and mines. In step with the expanding towns was the realization of the long-held dream of an education system and schools for all.

People have never been as materially affluent as they are today: no one walks barefoot to school. At one level, urban life is sophisticated, complex and rich. At another, however, it is deeply troubled and riven with doubt and uncertainty. The industrial economic and educational base upon which modern towns were constructed has fractured. The coal mines, steel mills and manufacturing industries have been decimated and replaced by information and high-tech industries which have different economic, social and educational demands. With these changes, the heart and spirit, as well as much of the urban geography of the industrial age, have gone. It seems that, as yet, there is nothing of substance with which to replace them.

This problem is compounded by the fact that throughout the growth and decline of the industrial age the role of both central and local government expanded substantially. Worthy citizens and the modern political parties tried hard to alleviate the harshest effects of the dark satanic mine and mill. They sought to plan society more effectively and to build a socially sensitive welfare state which took care of all its citizens. Material progress and the growth of urban areas coincided with the growth of government

bureaucracy, which came to influence most areas of life – housing, the family, education and health, as well as the economy.

However, industrial progress, the nature of towns and the welfare state have unintentionally undermined and weakened the social, moral and spiritual framework which people need to sustain the integrity and moral quality of their lives. The family, community, church and a host of voluntary organizations have withered on the vine. There is little which now mediates between the individual and the State or which can help people to withstand the pace and pressure of change.

The destructive consequence of this development was not at first apparent, for it was masked by the influence of the welfare state. It took on from the Church, family and individuals the responsibility for the care of others and absolved them from choice, blame and duty. Crudely, it could be asked: 'Who needs a family, neighbours and a sense of personal morality when the State can take care of all ills?' In the Eastern European communist states this question was answered with ruthless affirmation and application. In the UK it was mediated by the checks and balances of democracy, although the outcome for the individual and community has not been significantly different.

In effect, the welfare state institutionalized the vital human qualities of care and neighbourliness. For St Paul, charity was the fundamental building block on which the family and social life were constructed. In recent times it has become a ridiculed, socially peripheral concept which only the do-gooding Lady Bountiful might pursue in her spare time. When so few know who their neighbour is it becomes difficult to practise neighbourliness and to 'do unto others as you would have them do unto yourself'. Today the Good Samaritan walks by on the other side of the road. Materialism and the protective bandage of the welfare state have been applied so tightly to social relations that they have gradually cut off the vital, life-enhancing flow of blood to the fabric of life. The isolation and loneliness of the individual, the insecure street, the dispirited environment, the fractured and powerless community, a distrust of authority, the lack of hope and the urban riot are the results.

Thus, at the very moment when metropolitan sophisticates and the political parties claim that modern society has achieved real progress, most people, especially those who live in outer and inner city areas, recognize that society has become seriously flawed and that a quite different way of arranging social affairs is urgently needed before the downward spiral of industrial decay creates cities in Britain whose ills compare with those of Los Angeles. What for a long time has been understood, felt and articulated by those who live in the inner and outer urban areas – that something has gone seriously wrong with social life – has only recently been driven home to society as a whole by a welter of bad news, riots, crimes and poor educational standards which disfigure the face of the media and sap the spirit of the nation. People have protested between general elections by voting for the Liberal Democrats. However, they do not yet feel that any party offers a soundly based, alternative vision. The party which can break free from the past and offer this vision will command real authority.

This book thus attempts the painful task of pointing out that the heroic construction of the welfare state and structure of government have led to such unhelpful unintended consequences that their influence must be diminished and their powers refocused. Fresh, more robust and meaningful ways of organizing schools, communal and political life must be rapidly constructed if serious problems are to be avoided.

Part 1

The Problem of Urban Decline: Charitable Urban Solutions

Residents from inner city areas and outer city housing estates complain bitterly about the quality of their lives in a way which strikes a familiar chord with all city-dwellers. Just what is their problem and what caused it?

Can effective solutions be identified? Once identified can these be applied easily and painlessly or are fundamental changes to the nature of urban and social life required? If so, what factors, if any, might precipitate the will and political conviction to make the changes?

represent the culmination of social and material progress, but the crisis which they now face reveals to all that they are no longer adequate nor moving in the right direction. It could be that the last few years of the twentieth century herald an exciting new dawn as new local institutions and fresh political vision help a post-industrial society to emerge from the despair of industrial decay.

REFERENCES

Davies, B. and Anderson, L. (1992) *Opting for Self Management*. London: Routledge.
Osborne, D. and Gaebler, E. (1992) *Reinventing Government*. Reading, MA: Addison-Wesley.

communities and towns are organized, and the way we think about social relations in post-industrial society.

Chapter 12 discusses the idea of the urban village through which the many neighbourhoods which exist within each town can reassert their identity upon the urban landscape. A school or cluster of schools which is owned by the community, not imposed upon it, can play a crucial part in defining and asserting this identity. In gaining control of their own institutions it is likely that people will find pride and purpose in life. A fresh relationship between the individual and the State may be in the offing, with the individual and free-standing institutions making a more robust contribution and the State playing a more distant, though rigorous, enabling role. The implications of this development for the State, the political parties and the theories through which they form their policies are substantial. They are discussed in Chapter 13.

The Labour Party emerged at the beginning of the twentieth century as the champion of the working classes and their trade unions; the producers and makers of goods which only the owners of the means of production could afford to buy. It swiftly pushed the Liberal Party into third place and harried the Conservatives into helping it to build the egalitarian welfare state. It felt that individuals could only be helped by collective action rather than by their own endeavour. This view may have held substance yesterday but it has little purchase on today and will become increasingly out of synchronization with the kind of society which people need tomorrow. Throughout the 1980s Mrs (now Baroness) Thatcher and her friend, Ronald Reagan, successfully broke the collectivist consensus of the industrial welfare state with the help of the theories of the radical right and by appealing to the growth points of post-industrial society. Their successors now struggle to pick up their mantle. They flounder in an attempt to turn the harsher legacies of these radical years into a more caring, one-nation, conservatism.

The British Labour Party and the American Democrats were wrong-footed by the Thatcher and Reagan years and the changes they witnessed. In America, the Democrats began to find their feet with the help of Bill Clinton and the advice which Ted Gaebler and David Osborne offered in their impressive book, *Reinventing Government* (1992). Unless the British Labour Party can also swiftly find new bearings, a new way of seeing social life and advocating and supporting the growth points of society, then it is likely to add to the urban problems of which people complain rather than solve them.

Chapter 13 looks at the powerful collectivist theories which developed over the last 150 years legitimizing the growth of towns, government bureaucracy and the policies of the parties. These theories compete with and obscure those which facilitate radical, independent, grass-roots developments and they make fresh thought difficult. Chapter 14 outlines the new academy which is needed to help with the task of making social thought congruent with contemporary reality and to help the modern teacher, professional and politician discover the skills needed to run independent local institutions in partnership with new forms of enabling governments. It is not just the control of education which needs to be devolved from the town hall to the many urban villages which make up each town. Most functions are best devolved to the village if it is to develop the responsibility needed to play an essential role in the regeneration of urban areas. The proposed academies could play a key part in training the people who will shape the future style and purpose of towns, as well as the attitudes and actions of the political leaders of tomorrow.

The great urban areas took the last 200 years to build. Many tend to think that they

top-down responses of successive governments to the urban crisis before examining the voluntary, bottom-up responses which people in communities have themselves made. Chapter 4 focuses on one inner area of Birmingham, Balsall Heath, and the development within it of St Paul's charity. Balsall Heath and St Paul's are highlighted as 'ideal types' which stand for hundreds of inner and outer city communities in various parts of Britain. They illustrate how a local charity and local people can begin to reconstruct their own independent social and educational institutions and recover their pride and ambition.

Chapter 5 notes the universal characteristics which confirm that the residents of Balsall Heath are not unique but typical of those living in most cities. It examines the economic and social trends which have persuaded government to begin to devolve power and finance from itself to people in communities. Chapter 6 studies the educational reforms which the British Government introduced in the 1980s, culminating with the Education Reform Act 1988 and the White Paper of 1992 and the resultant legislation in 1993 which encouraged governors and parents to vote for their neighbourhood school to opt out from the grip of the educational bureaucracy of the town hall and become self-governing. As more sets of local people take ownership of their school in this way they demonstrate, first, that every area can come to shape its own institutions and, second, that there is no need to be dependent on institutions and services supplied by government.

It is possible that British society is at the beginning of a great sea change. Over the later part of the 1990s many state schools are likely to become independent from the town and county hall bureaucracy (hereafter referred to as town hall) which for decades was their controller. They will become devolved to, and controlled by, governors who come from the catchment area of the school. The education departments of each town hall and their committees of councillors will disappear and a quite new way of organizing and motivating schools will arise. The repercussions are enormous both for schools, the communities in which they are embedded, and for the Government and political parties.

Chapters 7, 8, 9 and 10 look at the potential of these new, independent, community-governed schools, the curriculum which they might develop and the new kind of teacher who will be needed to staff them. It also studies the new phenomenon of small groups of schools clustering together to share the virtues of independence and providing each other with a range of support services. These new schools are likely to develop community enterprise centres which will not just be of assistance to the school but also of value to the surrounding community. Because these reforms have been introduced by a Conservative Government and many town halls are Labour-controlled there is a deep suspicion about both the intention and outcome of the reforms. Do they constitute 'privatization' by the back door? Some are resisting the reforms. The outcome could be conflict and tension between the old system and the new, particularly because the Government has not seen or spelled out all the caring and democratic consequences of its action, only the competitive ones. A two-tier system of town hall-controlled schools and new independent state schools could arise. The fears of the left could be fulfilled, partly as a result of their own action. However, Chapter 11 argues once freed from the dogma of the Conservative right, the reforms can be urged in a genuinely fresh, radical direction. Any or all of the main political parties could benefit by grasping the opportunity which devolution and self-government present for transforming the way schools,

The problem and the urgent quest for solutions are not unique to Britain. Throughout the industrially developed world unpopular governments are asking: 'How can services be most effectively and appropriately delivered to communities in such a way that they are made more cost-effective, less, not more dependent on the central state supplier?' Many are beginning to shy away from established top-down solutions which entail the ever more expensive and extensive supply of these services by collectivist central and local government bureaucracies. By force of past industrial economic and educational necessity, it is becoming acceptable to explore the rich potential of a bottom-up approach in which communities themselves become revitalized through direct participation in the provision of their own services. The implications for the way the whole of society is organized are profound. Can the industrial town, its culture and mode of educational, social and political organization be sustained into the post-industrial era? Or is a key cause of the urban crisis the fact that society has become so top-heavy and unbalanced with the clutter of the industrial age that it needs to be radically restructured before it can recover a stable, post-industrial equilibrium?

Schools make an important case study. If schools are vibrant, producing good results and both high-achieving and well-motivated young people, then the community must benefit. If, however, they are failing to do this because they relate to the economic needs of the industrial past, then a community which is already in flux and uncertain of itself may decline further. This book, therefore, focuses primarily on the supply of schools to the community. If existing schools are failing, why is this so? How can poor schools be turned into good ones? Some supporters of the existing 'system' insist that the answer lies in the allocation of extra resources. They say that the welfare state does not care or provide enough, that it should spend more on the existing kind of school and, by implication, make the role of central and local government more important. Such people argue for more, not less, government.

Elsewhere in the world dramatic solutions are being devised, nowhere more so than in Russia and the old communist states, which are desperately trying to unlock not just a centralized educational system but also an economic and political one. However, such social democracies as Australia and New Zealand have jettisoned their large urban education authorities and set up a mechanism by which schools are locally managed. Similarly Belgium and the Netherlands are experimenting with a 'greater school-based independence', as Davies and Anderson (1992) explain. They also point to interesting reforms in Canada and parts of the United States of America. None of these, however, are potentially as 'radical as the grant-maintained movement' of new independent, state-funded schools in the United Kingdom. What are such schools like? Does the government policy stem from an 'elitist and divisive Conservative philosophy' or does it have real substance which can stand independent examination and the test of time? Can the new schools make a serious contribution to the solution of the urban crisis, as post-industrial society tries to find a reason and culture with which to endorse its existence? If the control and management of schools are to be removed from the structure of government does this means not more but less government or does it imply a different kind of government and a more sophisticated kind of democracy?

It is not possible to answer these questions and consider solutions without first acknowledging and looking realistically at the problem. Chapter 2 details the depth and range of the social ills which face Britain's urban areas. Chapter 3 turns first to the

THE LUNAR SOCIETY

In 1789 a group of men met regularly to reflect upon the cultural and social issues which were to place Birmingham at the centre of nationwide social and economic changes (see Simon, 1960). These changes heralded Britain's peaceful, social and industrial revolution. They led to the world we know and are anxious about today. Walking to these meetings in the light of the full moon, these men titled themselves the Lunar Society. Their members included Matthew Boulton, who created the Soho Company which sold 'power' to the world; James Watt, who devised the steam engine; Joseph Priestley, who discovered oxygen; Erasmus Darwin, a doctor and poet; and Josiah Wedgewood of pottery fame. Birmingham's major historian Robert Dent (1894) wrote about the society:

> What a wonderful assemblage it was! Here were gathered together the dreaming philosopher and the level-headed man of business, the chemist, the botanist, the poet and the wit, the mechanician and the artist, the scholar and the dilettante.

Regretting that his medical practices too often kept him from attending the meetings, Erasmus Darwin exclaimed: 'Lord! What inventions, what wit . . . will be on the wing, banded like a shuttlecock from one to another of your troop of philosophers.' Erasmus Darwin, grandfather to the even more famous Charles Darwin, imagined that James Watt's inventions could lead to dramatic further inventions:

> Soon shall they arm, unconquered steam! afar
> Drag the slow barge, or drive the rapid car;
> Or on wide-waving wings expanded bear
> The flying chariot through the field of air.

In 1889, just a hundred years later, Birmingham was granted the recognition and status of a major city by Queen Victoria and the first aeroplanes were on the drawing board. The inventions and creations of the men who devised the Lunar Society were recognized in that year to have helped to build modern Birmingham. It is also clear that these local people made a major contribution to the forces which shaped the rest of the country and, indeed, the industrial nations of the West.

Two hundred years later, in 1989, Birmingham celebrated the centenary of its recognition as a city. Unfortunately, the bicentenary of the Lunar Society passed with hardly a mention. Yet surely a contemporary challenge now calls out to be turned to advantage as an opportunity for the future. How can Birmingham and other urban areas which were built over the last 200 years to house the once trail-blazing, now fading and dated, industrial and manufacturing needs of a nation adjust to the new human, social, economic and cultural needs which beckon from the twenty-first century? Where are the men and women who could be assembled from the four corners of each city to look ahead and build towards the year 2089?

J. H. Muirhead, Professor of Philosophy at Birmingham University wrote in 1909 that the great men of the Lunar Society 'were agreed in everything but opinion'. He stressed this 'wholesome recognition of the insignificance of theoretical differences in view of practical agreement on the great ends and issues of life'.

Two hundred years ago Joseph Priestley, James Watt and friends asked: 'If the medieval way of ordering society no longer satisfies our needs, what can we put in its place? Given the rapid changes which are taking place to establish a new order, how can we harness and influence affairs? What kind of new schools do our children need?'

The rapidly changing face of today's urban areas requires that a modern version of these questions is posed. Do we not need a new economy, culture, architecture, style of education and arts, a new way of governing our civic affairs? J. Basset's proud description in 1812 of the Soho works in Handsworth, which Watt and Boulton had built, proclaimed that, 'All nature smiles around – there stands Soho! Soho! – where genius and the arts preside, Europa's Wonder and Britannia's Pride'.

What examples of innovation exist today or could exist tomorrow which will provide the building blocks of a new urban society? Will they comprise only new scientific and technological discovery, the ever more sophisticated refinement of the silicon chip? Or, is a new style of urban life also called for if the great urban areas are to be rebuilt and standards are to rise in communities as well as in schools?

It is doubtful that such a rare and select trail-blazing band of citizens can again be assembled as those who once walked to their meetings by the light of the moon. Yet the changes which led to the end of industrial society and which introduce the post-industrial age are no less profound than those which the Lunar Society discussed. The proposed academy is of such vital importance that we need not just one modern equivalent but many. The questions they must ask and answer with clear practical results are, in their own way, just as vital as those posed 200 years ago.

How can we live with the results of the industrial revolution? How can we fashion a new kind of urban age which does more than just pick up the pieces of the past but also rearranges them into a new and distinct post-industrial identity? Those who walk to the city's Lunar Society of tomorrow will surely become preoccupied with some of these concerns:

- Neither the medieval priest nor the modern sociologist has contributed the last word towards understanding the individual in society. The priest wanted to improve the individual by persuasion to choose good against evil and threatened the sanction of hell if he or she failed to make the correct free choice. 'Society' and 'social structure' did not feature in the priest's analysis. On the contrary, the modern sociologist denies individuality and choice and thus wants to help an individual to become perfect by altering and improving the determining 'social structure' of society. Today, however, it is clear that we must redress the balance between these two opposed and apparently irreconcilable views. On the one hand, like the priest, we must again appeal to an individual to reform and improve his or her conduct and place less faith in the mere reform of society. But, on the other hand, we must not throw out the collectivist baby with the sociologist's bathwater. For people's social circumstances influence the context and manner of their choices. People and the collective circumstances which surround them are in a dynamic, interactive relationship with each other. People make their own circumstances and are influenced by them. Any social theory which leans too far in the direction of one or other factor is likely to misjudge the realities of life and to make impractical proposals which impose upon an individual rather than to make choice easier.

  Max Weber pointed out that in order to develop, technological society had to demolish one kind of social structure – traditional authority – which gave people

the secure springboard of community and value on which to base their choices. It has created in its place a featureless or 'mass' social structure through which people suffer from what Emil Durkheim called 'anomie'. Without the props of family, community and traditional authority to rely on, people are more likely to become isolated and threatened. They become less able to make firm and coherent choices of the kind which will benefit both themselves and their neighbours. Vandalism, crime, social irresponsibility as well as general unhappiness have been the almost inevitable result.

- There is a natural and inevitable hierarchy of authority to the relationships between people. When this hierarchy becomes too complicated and unbalanced, because it is abused by those at its apex to further their own advantage, then those at its base who are subordinate may object. In taking the side of the subordinate, some politicians have encouraged people to defy authority. They have not appealed for a fair or new kind of authority but for no authority at all, which has resulted in a false equality which ignores the natural and necessary distinctions in life. The revolt against the dictatorial abuse of authority can merely lead to permissiveness and the breakdown of consensus. When political parties take sides on these questions – one with those who wish to retain their authority, the other with those who wish to oppose it – then they can inadvertently destroy the basis upon which social harmony is built by making it difficult for people to see that the proper use of authority is in the essential interests of both partners in the relationship.

- How can people who are located in different positions in the hierarchy and the different political parties all be helped to advocate and trust in the benefits which can come from a new and well-organized authority structure? How can that structure be protected against the ravages and rapid changes of a technological society and the conflicting theories of opposed political parties?

- The family is under very real threat and unless it is protected, the individual will suffer. This will have serious consequences for the rest of society and make it difficult to achieve the cohesive authority upon which social harmony depends. How can the family be strengthened and parents helped? How can good parenting skills and practices be encouraged? How can bad ones be discouraged? No doubt a variety of measures can be devised and put into place, but, it may well be that a number of legal reforms are also necessary.

- Communities are also under threat, so they also need to be supported and helped to become resistant to these threats. Such support may well include the provision of high status and rewards for those who are at the forefront of the redevelopment of communities either because they are at the grass roots or because they are enlightened, new-style, city and government planners.

- Do attractive universal values exist from which everyday codes of conduct, rules and standards can be derived which legitimize and support family and communal life? Can these help the individual to withstand the instant gratification which rampant technology offers and to choose in its place a more measured and morally superior alternative? Instead of searching for new and as yet unthought of values, is it possible to resurrect tried and tested traditional ones in order to assist with the stewardship of the social and material world? How can these affirm and reinforce standards and moral codes which are otherwise in danger of being confined to the periphery of society?

- The defining features of the technological society we live in present a dual threat which makes it more difficult for people to live contented lives in harmony with their fellows. Key elements of this society disrupt the 'social patterns and idea patterns on which a stable society depends', wrote Gordon Rattray Taylor (1975) in *How to Avoid the Future*. He points out that because material progress depends upon a high rate of innovation:

  it makes life unpredictable, renders projects obsolete long before the end of their design life and makes social adaptation (which is tied to the generation interval of human reproduction) hopelessly difficult. [Would it not be wise to reduce the innovation rate? For, a society] organized for conspicuous consumption and rapid resource use . . . [is] socially unworkable.

- It, therefore, seems impossible to have all the material benefits which a technological society brings and, at the same time, to retain social harmony. So, it is necessary to think hard about what is needed to reassert that harmony while retaining as many of the essential benefits of material progress as possible.
- If family, community and natural authority are to be strengthened, then not only must all young people be well-educated but all also need to be able to find fulfilling work. Yet, the loss of manufacturing jobs has not been compensated for by a sufficient number of new technological ones. How can full employment be sustained in a post-industrial society?
- The sophisticated requirements of a good education for all pupils will prepare both girls and boys to undertake a variety of different skilled jobs as they move through life, whereas their fathers only had one manual job and their mothers tended to the home. However, the new generation must also be prepared for prolonged periods of enforced unemployment unless government and other agencies find new ways of creating work in the ravaged communities of the land which are rewarding and economically productive.
- Some speak of automated factories which produce most of what society needs by remote control, supervised by a handful of managers who work for just a few hours from home while most people live a life of 'leisure'. This brave new world is not attractive to many. Man may not live by bread alone, but bread is a vital basis on which to build the energy which informs, graces and enlarges the spirit. Man is a working animal. How can the economics of technology and private enterprise become balanced by the economy of full and productive employment?
- The pace of modern life must somehow be slowed. It cannot be right that invention, trend and material affluence suggest to the impatience of the younger generation that its social and moral knowledge has moved ahead of that of the older generation. It really is necessary to 'honour thy father and thy mother', and to respect and revere the knowledge of grandparents and the elders of society. Otherwise, a rootless and directionless generation will result which cannot balance the inherited wisdom of the past with the fresh insight of youthful maturity.
- The brakes can only be applied in a way which carries conviction for the young if this is done firmly and fairly. Any failure to exercise responsibility is unlikely to gain respect. Rather, it may be seen as abdication and a licence to disregard rules. Can a change of pace also convince the innovator and economist?

- How can the increasingly popular concern with caring for the environment be more effectively advocated? How can the innovator enable this perspective to become more enconomically attractive?
- The combustion engine was a marvellous and profitable invention, but the private car and the road which voraciously eats both countryside and winding urban streets are unhealthy and wasteful. So, in the interests of the economics of health and the collective good, can motorists be persuaded to curb their rights in favour of public transport and pedestrians?
- Once cars as well as pots and pans lasted for a lifetime. Furniture and silver became heirlooms and were passed from generation to generation. Now, the family silver has been sold and disposable goods are manufactured for the mass consumer society. How can the craft skills of previous generations be preserved and made economically inviting?
- The industrial society and town of yesteryear was typified by pyramid-like organizations which provided standardized goods and services for people. This approach is no longer practical or efficient. A new world of choice, high expectation and instant information is creating new maypoles.
- Just what are the implications of the maypole for a new breed of DIY workers and agencies? How can those who used to both steer and row enable a whole new generation to row and contribute to the process of steering? The technology of post-industrial society provides such instant information through television and computers that whole populations now know as much as, if not more than, their employers and political leaders.
- The possibility of quite new forms of democratic practices arises. The democracy of the small Greek city state was limited only by the number of its citizens who could squeeze into its central arena. Today, the large populations of modern towns, even nations, could participate in a similar way if linked via computer – and if the politicians could be persuaded to loosen their grip on the reins of power.
- We noted that the Conservative Governments of the 1980s and early 1990s in Britain tended to respond to the need to abolish national pyramids by simply 'privatizing' them and introducing the competition of the marketplace. While they were right to tackle the problem which they inherited from the industrial age, the solution they imposed revealed major flaws. For example, schools could not simply be given 'independence' and left to compete with their neighbours in isolation from the town hall. They needed to find new ways of cooperating with their neighbours and they needed a new kind of authority, not simply to abolish the old one.
- Neither the social nor educational market can be simply compared with the business world, although they can benefit from many of its practices. Just what will this social and educational market look like? What demands will it place upon the active citizen, not just 20 per cent of the population, but the full 100 per cent of it?
- Which urban village in each town might volunteer to become the educational, architectural and economic Poundsbury of that town? Just how can one blighted urban village be transformed into a model for the future which others will be keen to emulate?
- Which town might pick up the challenge of the post-technological era and move heaven and earth to change itself into the city of tomorrow?

- Can the school, the clusters of schools, the community forum and the development officer of each urban village really play the role outlined for them in earlier pages? If so, just what help will they require from a reformed local and central government?
- What shape will the new town hall assume and what is the future for local and national political parties?

Some of the radical solutions required to solve the problems facing urban areas are already clear to people working in or managing a host of voluntary and non-governmental agencies. Birmingham can boast of several in addition to St Paul's. So can most towns. Such agencies have been waiting in the wings for a long time. They must now prepare to enter and move to the centre of the stage.

Similarly, Hillingdon, Kent, Birmingham and other authorities have experimented with the devolution of services to neighbourhoods. Such developments are exciting but tentative; they remain the exception rather than the rule. Yet they were unheard of a decade ago, and things are now moving in the right direction. It is important, therefore, to draw the scattered bottom-up and top-down initiatives together and to form a more coherent and consistent policy with which people can enthusiastically identify.

Both central and local government have a leading role to play in formulating this vision and policy. So do voluntary agencies and self-governing schools. Indeed, the more both vision and policy are a product of shared thinking, the more will all concerned gain a sense of ownership and make them work. The proposed Academy will wish to act as the catalyst which triggers and accelerates this process.

Existing sociology departments, training colleges and politicians have much to answer for. Perhaps the fresh centres of training and academies advocated here can go some way to redress the balance.

REFERENCES

Simon, B. (1960) *The History of Education 1780–1870*. London: Lawrence & Wishart.
Taylor, G. R. (1975) *How to Avoid the Future*. London: Martin Secker and Warburg.

Chapter 15

Conclusion

Presently it will be the year 2000. The UK will have left the second millennium behind and the third millennium will have dawned. People in every village in every town in Britain will rejoice when Big Ben chimes in that unique New Year. It will hold a very special promise which will have been in careful preparation during the years which led up to it. The present, so to speak, is already pregnant with the new promise of that New Year. What secrets does that promise contain? Do they foretell of bold dreams or of fretful nightmares?

Some of the great towns of the USA hold a terrible warning for the future of Britain's urban areas. The ills of which the opening chapters of the book complain are nothing compared to what could happen. School gates and doors could become steel shutters which open only when the correct pass is shown. Armed police could patrol the corridors and frisk the visitors. Outside the gates, the environment could have so deteriorated that it becomes beyond anyone's ability to renovate. The fabric, the bonds, which weld stable families and communities together could become so weak that social life breaks down altogether. The downward cycle of decay could develop such a momentum of its own that it cannot be stopped. The riots which a few towns witnessed in the 1980s and early 1990s could become so familiar that whole areas and estates become sink, no-go territories for the dwindling number of people who can still cope. Horrendous? But very possible. In the midst of plenty we could be standing on the brink of a new dark age.

Driven by scientific discovery and the powerful pyramids of rational legal organization the industrial age scoured the earth for the mineral wealth which could fuel its manufacturing might. In so doing the appearance of the Western world was disfigured in a way which only the welfare state could remedy. Yet the cure had unintended side-effects. The traditional values which once ordered social life and gave it stability and coherence were weakened. The individual became frightened and alone as family and communal life disintegrated.

The challenge which faces government, educators and spiritual leaders today is to create a new way of caring for the social and economic needs of the population. Can the political parties of tomorrow empower local communities so that this task is achieved or will they vie with each other to preside over further decline? Can they

become part of the solution or will they become part of the problem?

Many would respond to a clear lead, as they yearn not for a dark age but for a Renaissance. Although there are a variety of St Paul's-like charities which are scattered in every town there is no clear banner under which they can unite. Furthermore, for every visible sign of stirring at the grass-roots level there are a host of invisible ordinary people who fret for a more fulfilling life, a secure, tidy and attractive environment and a caring community. They too would eagerly respond if only they could see a clear lead which they could follow. Which party, if any, is most likely to create the context in which solutions can arise? On the face of it, it does not appear that the Labour Party is any longer in a position to set the necessary agenda.

At the beginning of the twentieth century Keir Hardie became the first Labour MP. His election announced the dawn of Labour's golden age. In 1900 the infant Labour Party gained just 60,000 votes. In 1918 it secured over 2,000,000 votes. By 1929 its vote had risen to over 8,000,000. In the landslide parliamentary victory of 1945 it secured over 12,000,000 votes. Yet, by the last decade of the century and after four successive general election defeats people seriously asked if the party could ever again muster the support to form another Government. The working class and union base which had caused it to grow at the beginning of the century had been eroded by the end of it. Labour Party membership has rapidly become less and less representative of society at large. Almost 66 per cent of members work in the dwindling public sector. In 1992 only 5 per cent of members were under the age of twenty-five and, as Martin Jacques has pointed out, 'Labour now has little connection with the dynamic groups in society.'

For the first half of the twentieth century the Labour Party grew as the producers and manufacturing industries, the working class and their unions grew. Its support held steady in the middle part of the century, but when industry declined, Labour's base and support also went into steep decline and unless it can adjust swiftly and radically to appeal to quite new categories of people who represent the new growth points of society it is likely to experience a lingering and bitter death over the next decade or two. There are some people who will fight to save the party they love, avert its eyes from the past and point the way forward. The possibility of losing a fifth election in a row in 1996/7 and the thought of a lingering death could concentrate the mind. Thus, in December 1992, John Smith, the leader of the Labour Party, announced that Labour was to begin a fresh look at Beveridge and the welfare state in preparation for the next election. He said: 'We should no longer be thinking just in terms of providing a safety net, but of creating a springboard to independence, self-reliance and personal fulfilment. People don't just want handouts, they want a chance to achieve.' Mr Smith has a difficult task ahead of him. It could be that the history of the Labour Party will prove to have been inextricably related to the waxing and waning of industrial society and that quite different, new, radical political forces and ideas will arise to take its place in the post-industrial era.

In stark contrast to Labour's (perhaps) terminal problems, the 300-year-old Conservative Party, which is nothing if not adept at survival, found fresh impetus in the 1970s and 1980s. Partly because it was less cluttered with collectivist dogma and theory it was able to adjust pragmatically to the needs and spirit of the times. Indeed, it anticipated those needs and led from the front. It first began to dismantle the sacred cows of a centrally organized economy to which it had previously subscribed along with Labour. Then, it turned its hand to public housing, the health service and, finally, to

education. Its reforms presented people with the possibility of constructing new, more caring institutions in place of those of the State.

In 1992 Douglas Hurd argued that: 'There is now hardly an area of British life where Labour is not defending the old status quo ... Labour prefers to court the public sector unions and the established interests of the town hall.' In stark contrast, he pointed out, the Conservatives have stolen the challenging, visionary high ground. It is they who seek to 'empower citizens, decentralise decision-taking,' and to actively involve ordinary people more fully in shaping their lives. The contrast with Labour could not be more clear, or could it?

Some 'one nation' Conservatives may have identified the important role which the 'active citizen', self-governing schools and communities could play but they have not spelled out how they can be most effectively supported or what the consequences for existing social organization might be. Ministers have acted as if it was sufficient to simply lift the dead hand of LEA and town hall control from schools for all of them to immediately and energetically exercise independence as if to the manner born. The motives of the Conservatives have been questioned. Their policies could lead to division and conflict rather than radical change.

It is exactly at this moment that a new initiative could wrest the high ground from Douglas Hurd and his colleagues. Such a move could come from Labour or the Liberal Democrats. They could form a bold alliance and fashion a new, radical centre party, although the collectivist views of Labour might prove to be too entrenched to allow such a development.

The leader of the Liberal Democrats, Paddy Ashdown, understands better than either the Conservative or Labour Party leaders just what is entailed in the bottom-up approach to reinventing government. He and his party have invested much energy into trying to break the existing political mould. Just before his party gained substantial electoral victories in the local elections of May 1993, he wrote that we must

> change the culture of our politics into one that values co-operation as much as we now value confrontation. . . .
>
> We cannot solve this country's problems unless we can find a way of unleashing again the power, imagination and dedication that, despite all the years of centralization by governments of both parties, has survived in Britain's communities. The spirit of community is one of our most valuable assets. At present, it is being wasted, even suppressed. . . .
>
> We have to discover a style of government that frees our communities from the obstructions which prevent them from implementing the ideas that meet local needs. If this means a government that interferes less and enables more, then so much the better. . . .
>
> If only politicians were prepared to listen to, learn from and share power with the communities that make up our nation. That way, the problems might not seem so intractable as they sometimes do to those sitting on the green benches of the House of Commons.

Although some leading Labour and Conservative politicians privately agree with these sentiments, the nature of the two 'main' parties makes it difficult for them to say so in public, let alone to integrate such views into the policies of their parties. It is as difficult for the politicians to face the necessary process of culture change as it is for the old-style LEAs. Yet face it they must, if the parties are not to become increasingly identified by the electorate as a part of the problem. The Liberal Democrats could make a real breakthrough if the other parties remain unable to adjust. What better place for them to start than in the arena of education and community development?

Today, the quality and style of education is at the crossroads. Schools face a choice between two alternative routes. At first glance, the choice appears to be a simple one between continued dependence on an LEA, which they can't influence but which is familiar, and the self-reliance which comes from self-government, which is tempting but leads to uncharted territory. Once the technicalities of self-government are overcome such a choice should be easy. However, it is becoming impossibly complicated because the two options are each associated with the different policies of the two main political parties. Further, one option appears to uphold the role of local government while the other is felt to diminish it.

Thus, unlike Rab Butler's great reforming Education Act of 1944, which was seen as radical but politically uncontentious, the 1988 Act, the White Paper of 1992 and the 1993 Act are defined as highly partial. It is as if the autonomy of self-governing status and the dependence of LM status are two irreconcilable political moulds into which the rival parties and different levels of government are trying to squeeze schools irrespective of their actual educational needs.

The Conservative Government must carry some of the blame for this. It has clearly failed to tailor its policies to the benefit of all schools. It has appeared to abdicate the role of government altogether in favour of an uncaring educational market economy in which only the fittest can survive. Labour and the institutions of local government must also carry responsibility. They have responded negatively and defensively to government legislation, appearing to cling to excessively centralized bureaucracies. They have thereby helped to create the tension and conflict which they accuse the Government of introducing.

Not surprisingly, the movement towards self-government has been slow. Schools are tempted by the finances and freedom of independence but they hold back through a concern for their neighbours and a respect for local government. Far from speeding the process of change, the lack of clarity in the 1992 White Paper acted as a brake. The outcome could be a two-tier system of bold, big, self-governing schools versus LM/LEA schools. Just when the nation most needs the whole of its population to be well educated and all schools to become high achievers the old divisions between an elite 20 per cent and a disadvantaged 80 per cent could prevail.

To apportion blame and become involved in politically one-sided recriminations would be counterproductive. It would deepen divisions at the very moment when we need to find a way of breaching the dam of misunderstanding which holds schools back.

As with most arguments between rivals there is some truth on both sides. These must be highlighted. There are other truths which neither side has yet acknowledged. When these truths are rescued and put together a third, more congenial option can be constructed. This third road is paved with all the virtues of independence yet curbs them with a shared, neighbourly vision for schools which is, or ought to be, politically uncontentious except to the most dogmatic or ostrich-like.

The 1944 Act represented the last time that education stood at such an important crossroads. It is interesting to recall that it emerged from the coalition government at the time of the Second World War. The party which takes the popular radical middle ground today will strike a similar chord and achieve much. For a devolved state system of education could enable them to help:

• schools to become autonomous and self-governing agencies;
• communities to become empowered;

- fresh spirit to enthuse towns;
- local authorities and the political parties to become invigorated and re-focused.

If the patterns and culture of a century are to be put aside and a new culture is to develop from the efforts of schools like Baverstock and Small Heath, agencies like St Paul's and a host of other voluntary organizations, then it will be constructed from a number of key components. These include:

- The individual and the family. It is important to think bravely and hard, but not for long, about how the family can most effectively be supported.
- The urban village is the next component. It needs to have a clear and vital existence in its own right if it is to help the individual and family to gain identity and security and be a springboard for personal security.
- Apparently dated concepts assume a new importance: neighbourliness, responsibility and quality.
- The old central authorities which had come to focus on the town hall are most suitably devolved to the urban village. Whilst a few key functions can only be undertaken centrally, much of the day-to-day life of the community is best undertaken by local agencies which thrive within the community.
- Crucially, these agencies will include new self-governing schools and clusters of schools.
- These schools will form their own community education enterprise centres which will support both the schools and the community.
- A community curriculum will help teachers and pupils to combine academic and practical skills and to work directly with the community with the help of quality and practical support teams.
- The age-old conflict between private and public education is misplaced and unproductive. The rigour and independence of private schools is injected into and combined with state-funded but locally managed schools. The new state independent school and clusters of schools are the hub around which a newly invigorated community turns.
- A new kind of teacher is needed to help to build and run the new school and to train others who are needed to staff it.
- Other professionals in such fields as architecture and medicine need to develop similar community orientations and sensitivities to those of the teacher. All will be helped by the establishment of on-the-job training centres which will relate to a new academy of urban regeneration. These will not just train professionals and residents but bring them together and help them to use and gain awareness of each other's skills in real life situations.
- The wider community will wish to employ its own skilled officer to help it to articulate its agenda for action which the new-style city authority will help to resource and implement.
- This officer will be employed by a local forum of active citizens who are less concerned with party politics and more concerned with helping their neighbours. The role of the conventional parties will shrink away from the control of neighbourhood affairs, while at the same time the steering role of government will increase.
- The new approach to planning, development and politics requires that the century long domination of the theory of collectivism is jettisoned. The theory of

individualism and choice combined with community with which it must be replaced is not new. It has a history which reaches back to Adam and Eve.

- The above elements will not mesh together without the use of St Paul's own notion of charity. As if in anticipation of Erich Schumacher, St Paul wrote that unless people can shape their lives and give to others as well as receive then they lose their dignity and become dependent. If autonomous schools and other independent local institutions are the warp of a strong community then charity is the weft. It is important for the main political parties to recognize this and elaborate their theories and policies accordingly. Perhaps the economic and educational interests of the country will compel them to do so even if compassion alone is not sufficient.

- The provision of services to communities by welfare state monopolies was suited to industrial society and was a distinct advance upon an agrarian one. But Canada, New Zealand, the United States and other countries are now ahead of the field in discovering that a quite different way of organizing and delivering the essential caring services is necessary if a post-industrial society is to thrive rather than fall into disarray and conflict. Modern Britain could catch up and overtake these countries if its political parties combined to refocus the activities of the town halls, create devolved mini town halls, and give communities their head instead of posturing and attacking each other.

The picture is drawn of a federal city with a town hall which diminishes radically in size yet which plays the pioneering role of co-ordination thus enabling the urban village to assume an ever more important role as it gains the confidence and skills to run most of its own affairs. In future the community and town must decide between them what the priorities are for the construction of the urban environment of tomorrow.

Only one key building block remains before the list is complete and a new-style modern town can be constructed. Can a new or existing set of moral values be exerted which is powerful and practical enough to weld together the different elements of an alternative social order? If it is time for a new urban and social Renaissance then it is also time to assert an integrated set of values which recognize and legitimate its existence.

Max Weber (1968), the sociologist who helped us to understand the nature of bureaucracy and collectivism, drew very pessimistic conclusions from his analysis. He did not think a new value could arise to help to give meaning to a new kind of social life. As the nineteenth century drew to a close and the twentieth century took root he found himself staring at the unimpeded growth of the rational legal style of bureaucratic organization. The pyramids of rational legal authority, the British Empire and communism were still in the process of conquering the earth. The faiths and beliefs of countries in the four corners of the world were keeling over in the wake of those apparently unstoppable forces and becoming subordinate to their requirements.

Mikhail Gorbachov helped the citizens of the Eastern European States to achieve this impossible task of resistance by indicating that he would not use the tanks of collectivism to quell any uprising of popular, traditional opinion. Contrary to Weber's expectation no fresh value was required to inform the thinking and unleash the pent-up aspirations of these peoples. Their traditional views had been long, if discreetly held. No one in Hungary or East Germany or even Russia wanted to be ruled by puppets, whose strings were jerked from the Kremlin, with which they did not identify. Their

In the process they can teach each other to become better at performing their respective roles.

The century-long relationship and attitudes between the professional city supplier and the dependent school and community customer cannot be changed so swiftly, nor can the new school and community be born without the aid of a midwife. There is a clear need for carefully prepared, on-the-job discovery, and an action and training programme. Those residents and professionals who are the first students in the first clusters of self-governing schools will in turn become the mentors and trainers of those who will follow them.

The successful development of schools is interdependent with the regeneration of the community, so it would be sensible to base the training centres alongside each urban village community enterprise centre. Each city may require one regional centre of excellence which brings all good practice together and which tests and advocates the new vigorous approach. This leading training centre, or academy, is likely to assume a role which a teacher-training college or university might once have played, but in the hands of the academy, that role will be developed in real, practical situations and be independent of the educational establishment. It will provide schools and communities with the services which they say they need, not what others think they need. The key trainers in the training centres and academy will be the community education specialist and the community's own community development officer.

The urban village community school and training centre could and should become the focal point for the revitalization of the surrounding community. If lifelong education is to be of real significance, then it must entail returning skills, confidence and expertise from overconfident professionals back to the people. The bottom-up, top-down partnership which results should enable the town hall's own activities to be accurately targeted upon those aspects of the community which really do need assistance. City action must respond to the question: 'In order to provide the service the community customer requires, how can we most efficiently co-ordinate our departmental skills and resources to enable the delivery of that service?' As in the case of the skills and resources of the previously centralized LEA, the answer to this question is increasingly likely to be: 'By giving to the community some of those skills and resources needed to deal with the situation itself, because it can tune them more accurately, adjust them more sensitively and do the job more efficiently than the city'.

Many town halls in Britain have quite properly invested very large sums of money in rebuilding their decayed, crumbling city centres. In conjunction with central government, local town halls have made heroic attempts to recover from the decline in their manufacturing industries. New high-tech, post-industrial office blocks, hotels, convention centres and Post Office towers pay tribute to the energy and pride of the city fathers. However, unless a similar energy, attention and will is focused on the decaying, dispirited sprawl which surrounds these new centres and spreads to outer city estates, then these centres are at risk of becoming the ill-designed mausoleums of an industrial graveyard. The task of the proposed academies of urban regeneration is daunting. There is a powerful precedent.

Chapter 14

A New Urban Academy

Although there are many indicators in addition to economic ones which point to the new post-industrial society in Britain, most public sector professionals and politicians are not yet familiar with the theory and culture which are necessary to identify and legitimize them. Just as we discovered that teachers and parents need to unlearn old educational 'them' and 'us' instincts and become confident in a new partnership, so also residents, professionals and politicians need to go through a similar process before the new culture can emerge.

RESIDENTS' PARTICIPATION IN COMMUNITIES

The old, formal, one-sided relationship between professional and client is not appropriate in the context of community and urban revitalization. Parents and residents need on-the-job training in problem solving and establishing the development of their community. They need to gain the new experience of receiving the support of those professionals whose interest they have hitherto been unable to attract. Similarly, professionals and politicians have much to learn if they are to deliver their half of the bargain, and recognize that to be practical and effective in their specialism they need to encourage the participation of their clients. Both professional and client will benefit most if they forge these experiences together in real situations. Consider the playgroup which is run jointly by teachers and parents; the park which is designed, built and maintained by residents, an architect and city officers; the new self-governing school which needs teachers and the community to combine to run it; all concerned will learn much from each other in the process of pioneering these developments.

As students, many professionals experience college life and a professional culture which is remote from that of the urban village. Direct experience is needed, which is likely to be more attitude changing than the traditional statutory brief spell in a 'difficult' area. The training of both resident and professional should take place simultaneously during the process of helping their agency or neighbourhood to develop, so that both can see the difficulties and potential of each other's contribution.

values were but a long-held personal identity and pride which had been hidden from but not obliterated by external domination. People wanted their faith, their flag, their idiosyncrasies, their way of doing things no matter how nonrational these might be. Once they have recovered from the legacy of the past everyone expects that these countries will be effectively run and happier places to live in. Yet how much easier and more harmonious things might have been had the central authorities passed power to the federal units before people felt that they had to rise up and seize it. A legacy of trust and respect might then have arisen in place of one of hatred and fanaticism.

Traditional values have been asserted not just because they are attractive but because their human scale is demonstrably more able to motivate the individual than the giant, impersonal organizations which until recently dominated the modern world. Tried and trusted truths command loyalty and dedication. Whether in Leningrad or Liverpool, Bradford or Birmingham, ordinary people are saying: 'We deserve better than this parcelling out of the soul of which Max Weber and Prince Charles complain.'

Basic values will give meaning to and integrate the different components which are needed to assist with the development of urban villages in a modern society. Once people are armed with the courage and confidence which a boldly asserted, coherent set of traditional values provides then they can build a more balanced urban life. The churches alone cannot assert traditional values and make them credible. They must be joined by all who have authority – the new school, other professionals, the police, parents and politicians – until the whole community is enthused.

If only politicians could compete or combine not to foist their ideas upon an unresponsive people, but to unleash their aspirations, then the whole country could be galvanized into action. Sir Bob Geldof and charities like Children in Need have merely given us a fleeting glimpse of the hidden potential for good in the widow's mite, the giving and receiving of charity.

The overprotective bandage of centralized restriction and corporate care is already being loosened to allow flexibility of movement and red blood to reach the wounds which urban life has inflicted. In a thousand communities in Britain, as in other countries, the equivalents of St Paul's are striving to reach those impoverished parts of its social, economic and educational life which the welfare state had rendered hopeless and given up for dead. Twenty years ago, the origin and approach of St Paul's, like that of other charities, seemed to be so untypical as to be almost eccentric, let alone the pointer to a viable alternative which might show how most aspects of life in post-industrial society might be organized. Perhaps its time has come?

REFERENCES

Ashdown, P. (1993) *The Independent*, 5 May.
Hurd, D. (1992) *The Sunday Times*, 8 March.
Weber, M. (1968) *Economy and Society*. New York: Bedminster Press.

Index

Kennedy, John F. 44
Kent 47, 154
Kiernan, K. 12
Krier, Leon 121

Labour Party 5, 38, 47, 156, 157
Lambeth 12
LEAs 43–51, 61, 65, 66, 67, 98, 99,
    107–15
Liberal Democratic Party 2, 157
Liverpool 7, 9
local government 43–53, 107–16,
    116–30
Los Angeles 2
Lunar Society 149–50

McLuhan, Marshall 68
Manchester 15
Marx, Karl 130, 142
Midlands 15
Midwinter, Eric 21
Millar, Peter 134
mini town halls 116–30
morality 41, 140–1
Morris, Henry 58
Moser, Sir Claus 17
Moss Side 118
Muirhead, J. H. 149
Murray, Charles 15

Nazim, Dr 140
neighbourhood forums 128–30
  officer 128–30
neighbourhoods 5, 116–30
neighbouring clusters 96
neighbouring schools 96, 106
Newtown 9
New Zealand 3, 39
Nicholas Chamberlaine School
    99
'no-go' areas 14

Office of Population Censuses and
    Surveys 11
organization
  school 60–72
  society 137, 138
Osborne, D. 5, 125, 126, 127, 128, 129, 131
Outward Bound Courses 79

parents 39
parish councils 127–30
playgroups 23
Plowden Report 91
political dogma 48
political parties 19, 20, 40, 41, 42, 48,
    121–9
political theory 105–46
pre-school workers 87
Priestley, Joseph 149
projects 75–80
pyramids 49

Reader's Digest 17
Reagan, Ronald 5
residents 116–30, 147–8
Russia 3
Rutter, M. 40

St Paul 2, 4, 23, 139
St Paul's church 25
St Paul's church hall 26
St Paul's Community Education Project
    Ltd 23–35, 50, 81, 101, 117, 140, 154
  centre 32
  community development 33
  community education and resource
    centre 26, 27
  community enterprise centre 31, 32
  Heathan Enterprises 31
  Language Alive! 27, 28
  management 32
  nursery 26